D1060559

THE GENEVA CONFERENCE OF 1954 ON INDOCHINA

THE GENEVA CONFERENCE OF 1954 ON INDOCHINA

James Cable

St. Martin's Press   New York

First published in the United States of America in 1986

Printed in Hong Kong

ISBN 0–312–32097–3

Library of Congress Cataloging-in-Publication Data
Cable, James, 1920–
The Geneva Conference of 1954 on Indochina.
Bibliography: p.
Includes index.
1. Indochinese War, 1946–1954—Peace. 2. Geneva
Conference (1954) 3. Indochinese War, 1946–1954—
Great Britain. 4. Great Britain—Foreign relations—
1945–   . I. Title.
DS553.6.C33 1986   959.704′1   85–27907
ISBN 0–312–32097–3

For Viveca, as always

Contents

List of Illustrations

Preface

Transcripts of Crown-copyright records in the Public Record Office, the main source of this book, appear by permission of the Controller of HM Stationery Office and all otherwise unidentified references in the notes are to the files in which such documents are classified in the Public Record Office.

Another valuable primary source was the diary kept in 1953 and 1954 by Sir Evelyn Shuckburgh, who was Principal Private Secretary to the Secretary of State for Foreign Affairs during most of the period covered by this book. The author wishes to express his appreciation of Sir Evelyn's kindness in allowing him to read these diaries and to quote from them, as well as for other useful information and advice.

Sir Denis Allen, Mr R. A. Burrows, Lord Carr, Mr John Cloake, Sir John Figgess, Mr Terence Grady, Sir Donald Maitland, Sir Con O'Neill, Sir Anthony Nutting Bt, Mr John Priestman and Sir Andrew Stark were kind enough to assist the author with information and advice. Sir Denis Allen, Mr Burrows and Sir Evelyn Shuckburgh also read various chapters in typescript. Unless directly quoted none of them bears any responsibility for the book's opinions or statements of fact.

A particular debt of gratitude is due to Mr Michael Brown, HM Consul General at Geneva, and to his staff for their constant efforts in helping the author to track down contemporary photographs. The copyright owners of the photographs included in the book (identified in the list of illustrations) were not only kind enough to grant permission for their reproduction, but, in many cases, to make this possible by reducing their normal charges.

The author's debt to the writers of works previously published is severally acknowledged in the notes and bibliography, but is throughout great. So it is to those librarians who helped him find them.

Thanks thus too concisely concluded, a couple of explanations are needed.

Persons mentioned in the book are named as they were known to the author at the time, subsequent changes of style being briefly indicated in the index. Names, not only of people but of places, presented a further problem which has been summarily resolved. Reproduction of all the variant spellings to be found in contemporary documents would have been needlessly confusing to the reader and intolerably vexatious to the editor and proof-readers. Most contemporaries, for instance, gave Mendès France the hyphen his biographer assures us to have been incorrect. Oriental names exhibit even greater variety. Vietnam was, and still is, spelt in many different ways: as one word or two, with or without hyphens and diacritics. Since 1954 an entirely different method of transliterating Chinese characters into the Roman alphabet has emerged, and though still not universally adopted, has made many familiar names unrecognisable to the ordinary reader.

The principle followed in this book is to use a single spelling throughout for all proper names without regard to the idiosyncracies of the writers cited. The only exception has been for passages quoted in French (translated in end notes), where such variants as Genève or Londres have naturally been retained. The single spelling chosen is the simplest version familiar to English readers at the time, eliminating hyphens and the like and taking no account of subsequent changes: Cambodia, Chou en Lai, Formosa, Indochina, Pham van Dong, Siam, Vietnam.

JAMES CABLE

Introduction

'I have lived 78 years without hearing of bloody places like Cambodia.'—WINSTON CHURCHILL[1]

This is the story of the Geneva Conference of 1954 on Indochina. It will be treated here as an important episode in the history of mid-twentieth-century British diplomacy. In a broader perspective, of course, it is the merest incident in the continuing tragedy of conflict in Indochina. That has already lasted longer, involved more nations, had wider repercussions and perhaps reshuffled more coalitions than the Thirty Years War in seventeenth-century Europe. And the Thirty Years War, modern historians insist, was misnamed. It could equally well have been called the Hundred Years War. In Indochina too, the dragon's teeth were sown long before the half century that saw, we hope, the worst of their harvest, but the bitter reaping is far from over. Americans, Australians, British, Chinese, French, Japanese, Koreans may each single out certain months or years as the period of their involvement in actual combat: most of the indigenous inhabitants now alive have never known a time when there was no fighting in Indochina. Many of them never will.

These Cambodians, Laotians, Vietnamese, to name only a few of the indigenous peoples, suffered most, but the turbulence in Indochina spread more than ripples through the world. Distant governments fell from power, remote peoples were agitated, the quivering kaleidoscope of international relations early acquired and still in part retains a distinctively Indochinese rhythm to complicate its shifting patterns. Of the world's continents South America has so far been the least affected, but Africa not merely furnished many soldiers, but felt on its own soil – in Algeria and Angola and Ethiopia – the repercussions of those distant shocks.

On all this vast and crowded stage only a small circle will be illuminated – for the single year needed to pick out the diplomatic dancers who briefly diversified a grimmer drama. Their *entracte*

1

began – the choice is arbitrary – on 28 June 1953, when Joseph
Laniel formed a new government in France after a long ministerial
crisis aggravated by anxious discussion of the French war, then
nearly seven years old, in Indochina. The final pirouettes were
performed on 21 July 1954, when the Geneva Conference reached
what passed for agreement and that phase of the war came to an
end.

The spotlight will not, of course, be focused on Geneva alone. It
must range widely to follow the antics of the British performers.
Within its chosen period this will be an examination of British
attitudes towards the conflict in Indochina, of British motives for
promoting the Geneva Conference, and of the conduct of British
diplomacy, not only at Geneva itself, but in the various meetings,
discussions and confrontations that preceded the Conference and
continued, in different places, while the Conference was in
progress. For this examination the primary source will be the
official records of the British Cabinet, Chiefs of Staff, Foreign
Office and other British agencies, as they were released to scholars
by the Public Record Office in 1984 and 1985. These will be
supplemented by the recollections of surviving participants
including, at the moment of writing, the author himself; by
contemporary accounts in the press and by the extensive
published literature. British accounts and views will, where this
seems appropriate, be contrasted with some of the different
versions available in published material of foreign origin. But this
is neither an universal nor an impartial history. The picture it
seeks to paint is that perceived at the time by British politicians,
diplomats, soldiers, officials – and by the readers of British
newspapers. This is a specifically British view of British
involvement in a particular aspect of the Indochina conflict, just
as the author's earlier book, *The Royal Navy and the Siege of Bilbao*,
presented one aspect of the Spanish Civil War only as it was
glimpsed through naval binoculars.

There are three arguments for considering this a less parochial
approach than it may appear.

The first is essentially the thesis of this book. Without persistent
British efforts the Geneva Conference would never have been
held, allowed to continue or permitted to end in even the limited
measure of agreement actually achieved. The story of these
efforts, and of the opposition they encountered, is in fact the
history of the Conference, even if that history is presented from a

chosen angle and in a national perspective. A different outcome, moreover, would have had wider consequences. These might – the point will be argued in the Epilogue – conceivably have been either better or worse. At every stage in the unfolding history of international relations different options were always possible. The path through swamp and jungle has many ramifications, real or hypothetical. In 1953–54 British decisions neither averted ultimate disaster nor offered any plausible prospect of assured success. They merely produced a pause which might have been employed for reflection. In the largest sense they did not divert the march of history, but they delayed it and they gave it a different character. Even if British efforts did not produce a genuine opportunity for compromise (and the point is debatable), they certainly altered the nature of what hindsight has accustomed us to regard as the inevitable consequences of choosing a different course. Without the Geneva Conference and its indispensable British ingredient international history would not have been quite the same.

Nor would British history. Some of the repercussions, particularly the contribution made by success at Geneva to débâcle at Suez, will be examined in the Epilogue. But there is another reason for attaching extra importance to British exertions in 1954. They provided the last example of an independent British policy exercising significant influence in the resolution of a major international crisis. In 1954 Lac Léman, the lake of Geneva, provided an appropriate setting for Britain's swan song as a Great Power, an event surely deserving a specifically British analysis.

The final justification offered for the parochial approach adopted in the present work is that it is still too early to attempt a definitive account of the Geneva Conference or to assign to the events of 1953–54 their true significance in the evolution of the Indochina conflict. Much of the evidence needed is still not available. It will be a long time, if it ever happens at all, before the surviving documents from Cambodia, China, Laos, the Soviet Union and Vietnam fill the gaps in our knowledge of the motives or the conduct of some of the principal participants. The interpretation of this new testimony and the drawing of conclusions will not only demand a rare objectivity in some future historian – perhaps from Africa or South America – but may well have to await the unerring sentence of time and the end of a conflict that is not merely still active in Indochina itself, but a continuing influence on the policies and societies of a dozen major powers.

That ultimate verdict, however, will never be delivered, whether by historian or by computer, unless the foundations have meanwhile been laid, brick by partial brick. For history cannot be written, nor its lessons understood, without some sense of how the options looked to those who had actually to choose between them. From the British standpoint, this is the right moment to attempt that preparatory task. The documents, hitherto concealed or, at best, subjected to a selective and interested appraisal, have been released[2] while some of those who wrote them, or whose actions they describe, are still alive to assist in their interpretation.

Interpretation is needed because documents can be as misleading as tapes or memoirs or even memories. Interpretation, however, encounters two contrasting types of difficulty. The sooner it is attempted, the scantier is the evidential base and the stronger the bias of immediate commitment. Delay may produce a cooler analysis of richer documentation, but it also entails the loss of much oral testimony from death and the erratic distortions of senescence. Emotion recollected in tranquillity may be as much the essence of history as it is of poetry, but the moment that combines recollection and tranquillity is not easily identified, even if the choice were free – which it never is.

That is why the extensive literature devoted to the Indochina conflict – already surpassing in volume even that excited by the Spanish Civil War – offers such uncertain guidance. Most of it was devoted to the actual fighting or to the negotiations and political transactions of later years and much of it was more concerned to justify or to alter the course of events than to explain what had actually happened. The few serious works that focused on the Geneva Conference itself are mostly out of date.

Their obsolescence has deeper causes than the technical problems already mentioned. The Geneva Conference is one of those events which require periodical reassessment if their lasting significance is to be appreciated. Although diplomatic historians should always strive to depict transactions and decisions as these appeared at the time, hindsight is bound to influence the choice of what to describe, what to emphasise and what to treat only in passing. The hindsight of the sixties, when most of the existing books were written, was inevitably different from our own. Moreover, history is a didactic art and the writer who attempts it always has in mind the lessons which the past may offer for his own times. If we are no longer content to rely upon Gibbon or Macaulay or Trevelyan, it is not merely because lesser men have since challenged some of their facts or interpretations, but because the relevance of their conclusions has faded with the passage of time. Only literature lasts: history requires constant revision.

This provisional account of the British rôle in the Geneva Conference of 1954 is circumscribed in time and scope; selective in the choice and presentation of its material and deliberately British in its approach. It nevertheless needs a brief setting of the wider scene in order to provide the main story with its essential antecedents.

*   *   *

'The Vietnamese reached the Red River Delta two thousand or more years ago'[3] and, after a millenium as a Chinese province, achieved an autonomous kingdom in AD 939, not long after the establishment by Alfred the Great of an equally precarious kingdom in England. In the turbulent centuries that followed only a handful of isolated events directly concern the story of this book. In 1898, after fifty years of progressive French military encroachment, Paul Doumer consolidated French colonial occupation of what are now Cambodia, Laos and Vietnam by the imposition of direct rule in the Indochinese Union. As the United States acquired the Philippines in the same year, 1898 is a convenient date for the final establishment of foreign rule throughout South East Asia, with the single exception of independent Siam, now Thailand. Indeed, in all Asia east of the Khyber Pass only Siam, Japan and China enjoyed significant independence and China had to endure many constraints and encroachments on her sovereignty.

This remarkable and extensive ascendancy of white men, mainly Europeans, had been long in growing and, in its fullest extent and most absolute dominion, lasted little more than half a century. At the time it seemed, at least to white men, eternal and predestined, only liable to disturbance by conflicts, then endemic, in the natural centre of the world – Europe. Indochina, for instance, was at worst a potential source of dissension among European powers, particularly Britain and France.

This attitude was always an illusion. It should have been seen as such in 1905, when British battleships were withdrawn from the China Station and the security of the British Empire against external attack, not only in Asia but in Australasia, was recognised by the far-sighted as depending on the Anglo-Japanese Alliance. This dependence was emphasised in the First World War, when Japanese participation was the crucial factor in depriving Germany of her Asian colonies and Japanese tolerance essential to the survival of British, Dutch, French and Portuguese possessions. After that war the importance of Japanese power was generally admitted but, for a variety of reasons, neither American nor European colonialists could bring themselves to choose between alliance with Japan and organised opposition to her ambitions. Germany and Italy had no stakes on the Asian board and those of the Soviet Union were a geographical extension of her metropolitan territory. These countries could and did follow different and independent lines of policy and should not be reckoned as Europeans for the purpose of the ensuing arguments.

The fallibility of European calculations concerning the Asian balance of power was familiar and part of an established pattern. The twentieth century rise of indigenous Asian nationalism was a newer phenomenon. To begin with, it seemed a long term problem, a movement that would require eventual accommodation but that could meanwhile be controlled, moderated, canalised, from concession to compromise, into an evolutionary process culminating in the kind of society that would be compatible with a gradual withdrawal of white rule and acceptable when that withdrawal was complete. Between the wars that was the middle ground of informed, even enlightened, white opinion, though conservative Europeans (Churchill, for instance) wanted to retard, even frustrate, the process and radical Americans (such as Roosevelt) to accelerate it, at least in those mainland areas of Asia for which they had no direct responsibility. Most white men in Asia, of course, were less far-sighted, but there was a minority of sensible Europeans and Americans who tended to agree that evolutionary development was preferable either to an intransigent defence of the status quo or to revolution. Their differences were twofold. Most Europeans attached importance, as most Americans did not, to the ultimate retention of political links between even autonomous colonial territories and their former rulers. Most Europeans were more pessimistic than most Americans, both about the feasible pace of advance to Asian self-government and about the eventual ability of Asians to produce governments that would be either internationally acceptable or able and willing to serve the best interests of the indigenous peoples. 'The White Man's Burden' was no longer a respectable slogan, but the sense of obligation it implied was still an influence, particularly among those with any share in administrative responsibility.

The deliberate approach favoured between the wars by the conventional wisdom also reflected the relative ease with which European ascendancy was maintained. This was the period when 1300 British officials ruled 350 million Indians with the assistance of one British soldier for every 6000 inhabitants; when Rear Admiral Yangtse and his antiquated gunboats sufficiently reinforced the ability of British Consuls to preserve the security and privileged status of British communities hundreds of miles inside turbulent China. Prestige still gave authority its potency, no longer in the Kipling era, but in that of Somerset Maugham. He recorded, in his dispassionate manner, the ignominious dismissal of a British District Officer who had called for military reinforcements instead of quelling a riot with a couple of policemen and his personal authority.[4] Much was then expected, in Europe, of those described by an earlier Viceroy of India as 'a little foam on an unfathomable and dark ocean.'

In South East Asia there were naturally differences, apparent in practice before the Second World War and reflected in expectations after it, between the assumptions, the approach, the 'style' of one colonial nation and another. In 1945 these differences were overshadowed by a common failing: European perceptions were out of date. Whereas uninterrupted British administration had kept those concerned in London fully informed of the rapidly evolving political situation in India, South East Asia had been enemy territory for years and such intelligence as could be obtained was primarily military. This black-out extended even further. At one stage of the war HM Consul at Macao boasted of being the only British official at liberty for a thousand miles in any direction. In Indochina, admittedly, the Japanese tolerated a subservient French administration until 9 March 1945, but the assimilisation of their knowledge by the new rulers of France was difficult, not merely because of imperfect communications during the war, but because the Resistance-based government in Paris distrusted those who had stayed at their posts, either in Vichy or in occupied Indochina.

The attitude of most European decision-makers to the chaos of post-war South East Asia was thus predominantly influenced, not by recent political analysis, but by their own memories of a period when peace and order had been economically maintained by European administration, to the advantage of the European countries concerned and, arguably, to that of the great majority of the indigenous inhabitants. Having known better times, these European leaders were not inclined to accept the inevitability of worse. They did not, most of them, realise that the imposed order and authority of an earlier era had depended on a white prestige irretrievably swept away by Japanese triumphs and the following years of deliberate and systematic humiliation of Europeans and Americans before the gaze, at first astonished, then acquiescent, finally often approving, of the indigenous inhabitants of South East Asia.

Even those who realised that change had occurred did not consider it irreversible. It had been the mere by-product of war and wars, particularly to the British, had always meant a succession of disasters redeemed by final victory. They and their European allies also thought they had absorbed another lesson from this particular war: the ability of resolute leadership to survive disasters which became irretrievable only when accepted as such. American assistance had naturally been crucial, but they believed, as did many Americans, that the gods helped only those who had first demonstrated the ability to help themselves. Leaders conscious of owing their present ascendancy to their refusal to adapt to the brute force of adverse circumstance, to the part they had played in the heroic age of the early forties and in the later, but no less arduous exertions of European reconstruction, could sometimes be more romantic than realistic in their approach to what seemed the secondary problems of re-establishing colonial rule.

Anyone who had not seen for himself – and it will later be important to establish who did – the impact on the indigenous peoples of South East Asia of the astounding events of 1941–6 thus had more than one excuse for regarding Allied victory over the Japanese as the natural prelude to the restoration of something approaching the status quo ante bellum. In 1945 there would, in the best of circumstances, have been a chasm of mutual incomprehension between the returning colonial rulers and the emergent nationalist leaders of South East Asia. The former regarded the defeat of the Japanese as ending the interruption of colonial administration; to the latter Japanese surrender only confirmed the conviction established by Japanese triumphs: foreign rule, any foreign rule, was not merely undesirable but ephemeral.

Dispute was everywhere inevitable. That it so soon turned to conflict in Indochina and Indonesia was partly because these territories, unlike others in South East Asia, did not even owe to their former rulers the expulsion of the Japanese, partly because their nationalists had been given greater opportunities to entrench themselves. By the time French forces reached Indochina in strength, at the beginning of 1946, it was militarily too late for easy repression and, in terms of French politics, too soon for the alternative expedient of sweeping concessions.

The sad history of Indochina between the beginning of 1946 and the middle of 1953 is outside the restricted scope of this book. It may nevertheless be asked why these were years of continuing conflict between France and the Vietminh (the name given to the dominant nationalist faction in Vietnam). The British, after all, had conceded effective power to the Burmese nationalists as early as October 1946, even if Burma did not formally become an independent republic outside the British Commonwealth until 4 January 1948 (a greater degree of independence, incidentally, than that vouchsafed in 1946 to the Philippines by the United States). In Indonesia, after four years of sometimes successful fighting, the Dutch gave up the struggle in December 1949. Why did the French persist so long?

The general cause of mutual incomprehension apart, there were perhaps two main reasons.

The first was the need, intensely felt by many Frenchmen, to restore the 'grandeur' of France. Their country had not merely been conquered and its territory occupied and devastated: the rank and status of the nation had been called in question, particularly by Roosevelt, and the interests of France, in the Levant for instance, brutally disregarded by even her British allies. The knowledge that years of effort would be required for recovery at home only increased the importance of reasserting French authority overseas. The British, battered, impoverished but never humiliated and proud of their prowess in war, were psychologically capable of abdication, not merely in Burma but even in India, but this was then an option as politically unacceptable to the French in Indochina as it was to the Dutch in

Indonesia, who had also sought agreement in 1946 on terms significantly less than abdication.

If the French were also able to go on fighting longer than the Dutch, this was mainly due to the growing Communist ascendancy in the leadership of Vietnamese nationalism. This transformed the attitude of the United States, initially hostile to the reimposition of French rule, and not only spared the French the unremitting American pressure exerted on the Dutch in Indonesia, but, from 1950 onwards, ensured that French military efforts in Indochina were supported by ever-increasing financial and logistic aid from the United States. By June 1953, for instance, the United States were paying just under half the cost of the war.[5] Only such massive subsidies, to say nothing of aircraft, other equipment and technical assistance, kept the French able to continue the fight.

When the story of this book properly begins, in the middle of 1953, the French had been fighting Communist-led insurgents (Ho Chi Minh had always been the principal leader and he had been a Communist since at least 1920)[6] in Vietnam, with lesser repercussions in Cambodia and Laos, for nearly seven years. It was a war in which it was considered politically inadmissible to commit conscript forces (unlike the simultaneous British campaign in Malaya) and which made correspondingly disproportionate demands on the élite of the French Army as well as on African units and the Foreign Legion. It has been extensively described, but the busy reader seeking only the flavour, the character and the complex political environment of that war cannot be better or more easily enlightened than by Graham Greene's classic novel *The Quiet American*.[7]

In France this inconclusive struggle caused a would-be Prime Minister to tell the National Assembly on 3 June 1953: 'chacun reconnaît aujourd'hui qu'il est devenu impérieux d'alléger le fardeau que nous impose la continuation de la guerre d'Indochine'.[8] For the Americans, however, now that fighting had ceased in Korea, Indochina was the front-line in the Free World's resistance to the expansion of Red China. In British eyes the French were providing the forward defence of Malaya and Singapore.

Although the British and American governments had strong reasons of their own for wishing the French to pursue their struggle to a successful conclusion, both had serious reservations about its military and, still more, political conduct. They thought the French should be more whole-hearted, not only in the application of military force, but in their mobilisation of non-Communist indigenous nationalism by political concessions. Unfortunately the general tenor of their advice, more copious perhaps from Washington than from London, seemed to the French to be not only framed in ignorance of their domestic problems, but calculated to undermine just those national objectives for which, as it happened, they were actually fighting.

In the first half of 1953 it suited all concerned, from very different motives, to describe the conflict in Indochina as an international dispute. This was not in fact the case. Many governments had taken a public posture and a few had provided material assistance to one side or the other. But only France and the Vietminh were both principals in the dispute and actual combatants, directly and deeply committed.[9] The story of this book is one of the internationalisation of what had hitherto been an essentially bilateral dispute.

It might not have happened if 1953 had not seemed such an ominous year. It was the culmination of a long period of international tension, in which the United States and their European allies had felt themselves exposed to unremitting Soviet hostility, menace and pressure. One crisis had followed another in apparently escalating rhythm: Trieste, Communist insurrection in Greece, pressure on Iran and Turkey, the coup d'état in Czechoslovakia, the Berlin blockade, the first Soviet nuclear test, Communist victory in China, the war in Korea. Revisionist historians had not then questioned the central direction or the sinister pattern of these events. The shell-shocked Europeans of the early fifties lacked even the limited confidence which experience has given to their descendants. Threats, challenges, crises, confrontations, local conflicts were not seen as incidents in an enduring Cold War, but as the prelude to a real war that looked increasingly likely. Apprehension was more general and sustained than has been the case since 1962.

Such fears were not one-sided. The official history of Soviet foreign policy introduces its brief summary of the period which concerns us with a paragraph of mirror imagery.

'The formation of NATO, the US aggression in Korea, the arms race, and the militarisation of West Germany strained international tension almost to bursting point. US imperialism pushed its claims to world supremacy. Relying on their transient atomic superiority, the imperialist circles made preparations for another war, their objective being to destroy the socialist system, restore capitalism in countries that had rejected it, and suppress the turbulently spreading national liberation movement'.[10]

In London apprehension was generated by the hostility of the Soviet Union, but was not altogether allayed by alliance with the United States. The reasons were paradoxical. From 1944 onwards successive British governments had initially experienced some difficulty in convincing leaders in Washington of the need for American help in maintaining European confidence in the face of the Soviet threat. Now the boot was on the other foot. American reactions to Communist success in China and to the Korean War, particularly the difficulty experienced by President Truman in controlling General MacArthur, had aroused some alarm in Britain and prompted a much publicised visit to Washington by Attlee, then Prime Minister. In left wing circles, at least, the suspicion had since arisen that the United States were coming to accept the inevitability of war, a notion undoubtedly encouraged by the pronouncements of certain American senators, congressmen and publicists.

The British government, for their part, trusted President Eisenhower, elected at the end of 1952, the year after the return to power of his friend Winston Churchill. Eisenhower's experienced but doctrinaire Secretary of State, John Foster Dulles, was a less reassuring figure, whose public statements suggested that he envisaged foreign policy as an ideological crusade to 'roll back Communism'. There was nevertheless a strong disposition among British ministers and officials to believe that the good sense of their American counterparts would rise above the anti-Communist hysteria fomented by Senator Joseph R. McCarthy, chairman of the Permanent Investigations Subcommittee on Governmental Operations. The impunity with which that twentieth century Titus Oates had been allowed to slander statesmen so widely respected in Britain as General Marshall and Dean Acheson was thus a disturbing indication of the over-excited state of American public opinion.

The political climate in Washington also seemed to have blunted American receptivity to those early signs, which the British thought they had detected, of a change in Soviet attitudes. A detailed calendar of Soviet statements and actions since the death of Stalin on 5 March 1953, for instance, was circulated to the Cabinet on 3 July 1953 by Lord Salisbury (acting as Foreign Secretary during the illness of both Eden and Churchill).[11] There were no substantial concessions on major issues to record: merely repeated signs of apparent readiness to emerge from the total seclusion which the paranoia of Stalin's final years had imposed. The presence of Molotov, the Soviet Foreign Minister, at the Coronation Ball given by HM Embassy at Moscow on 2 June 1953 may seem a trivial instance, but it was a change in policy decided at the highest level and dutifully imitated by Communist diplomats, long used to rejecting all social invitations, throughout the world.

Neither this nor any of the other incidents listed indicated any lessening of Soviet hostility, though the Defence Committee of the Cabinet felt able to conclude on 14 October 1953 that general war with the Soviet Union was on the whole unlikely in the period up to the end of 1955[12]. All the signals suggested was that some contacts were again permissible, that discussion was possible and, so the British hoped, even negotiation conceivable.

If there was apprehension in the non-Communist world in mid-1953, there was also a spectrum of diverse opinions concerning the best approach to the innumerable unsolved problems, causes of dispute and potential flash-points that alarmingly diversified the international scene. The Americans led the hard-liners: ideologically committed; distrusting diplomacy and abhorring compromise; intent, so their critics argued, on the unconditional surrender of their adversaries. At the opposite extreme, among non-Communists, were the Indians: the intolerably high-minded advocates of woolly agreements that conceded everything unrelated to Indian national interests, of which they took an entirely selfish, but not always realistic view. The British, as usual, occupied the middle ground, sceptical alike of principles and of the possibility of general agreement, but usually willing to attempt the negotiation of particular issues.

One Briton who wanted to go further was the Prime Minister, Winston Churchill, then still recovering from his stroke, but soon to resume the pursuit of his final ambition: to negotiate a lasting peace at a Summit Meeting with the Russians.

Indochina did not figure in those dreams or rank high among the priorities of more orthodox Britons. Paris was the only major capital where Indochina headed the diplomatic agenda.

1 French Attitudes and British Expectations

'France is a sick country and only dynamic ideas and leadership can save her.'—HM EMBASSY PARIS[1]

These words were written on 24 June 1953 as the longest political crisis in the history of the Fourth Republic – it had lasted five weeks – was about to end in the formation of a new government. As André Siegfried later explained, there was no coherent majority in the predominantly right-wing National Assembly. Every time a government fell – a frequent occurrence – an ad hoc majority had to be cobbled together by the next coalition cabinet: not to support a particular party, but to endorse a programme embodying the lowest common denominator of diverse political objectives. This crisis had lasted longer than most because it had no single cause, only a multiplicity of conflicting grievances, some more urgent and important than others: 'trois questions fondamentales, mettant chacune en cause l'intérêt national . . . politique économique . . . l'Europe . . . l'Indochine, ce boulet qu'on traîne avec une impatience croissante'.[2]

Although we shall only be concerned with the millstone of Indochina, the French saw this both as a burden on its own and as the principal obstacle to the restoration of their economy and to the resumption of their proper rôle in Europe. The persistence of France's many problems also seemed to spring from the political system that condemned the country to a series of weak, short-lived and disunited governments. That was the long established view of General de Gaulle, then still in self-imposed isolation. 'La France', he had declared on 13 June 1953, 'n'est pas en train d'expirer', but her politics had to be remarried with the life of the nation.[3]

The British Embassy were not looking to that quarter for dynamic ideas and leadership. The candidate they favoured was

14

Pierre Mendès France, himself once a Gaullist, now a Radical deputy with a reputation for rejecting half-measures. Unfortunately he failed by 13 votes to obtain the necessary majority and the Prime Minister finally approved by the National Assembly on 26 June was Joseph Laniel, an Independent deputy who had never previously held any major office. The Embassy called him 'a solid and respected Norman with a good resistance record', but in the Foreign Office Miss Barley Alison dismissed him as 'uninspired and uninspiring',[4] a view evidently shared in France: 'the country as a whole regarded the whole business with a bored distaste'.[5]

M. Laniel's personality did not influence Sir Oliver Harvey, the British Ambassador in Paris, when he attempted to predict the future course of French policy towards Indochina (and other issues of importance to Her Majesty's Government). Because of the imminence of the Bermuda meeting (then scheduled for 8 July 1953) of the President of the United States and the Prime Ministers of Britain and France, his despatch had to be sent off on 26 June before the crucial vote in the National Assembly had decided who would represent France on that occasion. The Ambassador did not hedge his bets.

> It will be of no avail in my opinion to urge the French to make greater sacrifices and greater efforts whether in Indochina or in Europe. The reply will be that they are already doing too much.
>
> There are differences of opinion in the Assembly about the methods by which the defence burden could most conveniently be lightened. But there is a wide measure of agreement that it is in Indochina that the principal savings must be looked for.

He conceded that 'at present the Americans are paying for just under half the cost of the war', but he concluded:

> I would expect the French party at Bermuda to be more interested in discussing the possibilities of reaching a peaceful conclusion to the conflict than of [*sic*] considering whether fresh resources might be assembled to win a military victory.[6]

His despatch can scarcely have left Paris before Laniel, in his speech seeking the support of the National Assembly, had declared that France's burden in Indochina was too heavy for her to bear alone and that he would say so at Bermuda. He added – and he was the first Prime Minister designate to include such a promise in his programme – that he would make every effort to bring the war to an end by negotiation in agreement with the governments of the Associated States of Indochina. It is scarcely surprising that the Ambassador's gloomy predictions were broadly endorsed in the Western and Southern Department of the Foreign Office (which dealt with France) and by that Department's superintending Under-Secretaries.

Even Denis Allen, the Assistant Under-Secretary of State responsible for Asian affairs, did not question the Ambassador's judgement when he added his minute, on 1 July, to the others attracted by this important despatch. He merely argued that British policy on Indochina must be maintained, regardless of likely French objections, and every effort made to bring it to fruition. Lord Salisbury, whose appointment as Acting Foreign Secretary during the incapacity of Winston Churchill (who had himself assumed charge of the Foreign Office on 7 April 1953 because of Eden's illness) had been announced on 29 June, read both despatch and minutes, but recorded no comment.[7]

What was this British policy which had to be pursued in spite of the French? It had been formulated, again in preparation for the Bermuda Conference, in a draft brief submitted by John Tahourdin, Head of the South East Asia Department, on 24 June. This draft had been cleared, as was Tahourdin's prudent practice, not only with other departments in the Foreign Office, but also with the Chiefs of Staff. It was important, when putting forward views that might not only be unwelcome, but even attract the pejorative epithet – then in common use – of 'defeatist', to mobilise widespread support.

The views expressed were undoubtedly unwelcome.

The threat to UK and other Commonwealth interests in South East Asia, notably Malaya, increases as the position in Indochina deteriorates. With their present policy the French are drifting towards an eventual collapse. . . . Militarily the initiative rests entirely with the Vietminh. . . . H.M. Chargé d'Affaires in Saigon has expressed the view that in supporting the French effort as at present conceived we are backing an almost certain loser. H.M. Embassy in Paris share this view.

The French should thus be exhorted to change their policy: to encourage non-Communist nationalism in Indochina by giving the governments of the Associated States greater autonomy and to strengthen their own military effort by sending an extra two or three divisions to Indochina.

Approved as a brief for the Bermuda Conference, the draft was forwarded in final form on 25 June to the Prime Minister by Selwyn Lloyd, the Minister of State who had been running the Foreign Office, under Churchill's rather intermittent supervision, since 7 April 1953.[8]

It was thus a trifle disconcerting to find HM Ambassador at Paris, the very next day, insisting that the possibility of any French government being willing or able to send out two or three divisions of French troops to Indochina 'can be ruled right out.' Churchill might have suggested, in a House of Commons debate in May 1953, that the French should use conscripts in Indochina as the British did in Malaya, but 'the law does not authorize the despatch of national service men overseas ... except as volunteers'.

When it came to French policy, there was thus a clear disparity between what the Foreign Office in London considered desirable and what the Embassy in Paris regarded as feasible, let alone likely. British expectations were nevertheless more than a departmental obsession. Malcolm Macdonald, the United Kingdom Commissioner-General for South East Asia at Singapore – a kind of regional viceroy with ill-defined powers but considerable influence – had sent an emphatic telegram on 30 June. Although his political career early launched by one Prime Minister – his father Ramsay – had been prematurely terminated by another – Churchill, who disliked him – his diplomatic advancement had reached its zenith in Singapore. His luminous intelligence, his personal charm, his informality and absence of prejudice gave him an exceptional ability to understand and influence Asians. His indefatigable energy and enthusiasm, when not overwhelmingly deployed across the breakfast table, impressed his compatriots. On the whole this was fortunate, for he understood, as most of them did not, the nature and importance of Asian nationalism. But he was an optimist and he shared his father's tendency to exaggerate the merits of those most susceptible to his own charms.

Now his diagnosis and his prescription matched those of the

South East Asia Department and he too invoked military support (that of the three British Commanders-in-Chief for the Far East in Singapore) for his arguments. He emphasised the likely repercussions in Siam of any Vietminh success to point up the threat to Malaya and he spelled out the nature of the political concessions needed: a French declaration promising the Associated States, at the end of the war, the same status in the French Union as that enjoyed by India in the British Commonwealth. This would have to be publicly endorsed by the British and American governments if it was to be credible in Indochina, where 'French are intensely disliked and suspected . . . it is too late for them to recover their reputation by piecemeal reforms'.[9]

These Associated States for which greater independence was desired were Cambodia, Laos and Vietnam. The first two had kings and the third an emperor, His Imperial Majesty Bao Dai. Their prerogatives were circumscribed by French reservation to themselves in 1949 of responsibility for defence, foreign affairs, finance and the privileges of French nationals, but their position had been recognised – a little cautiously and at French insistence – by the British Government on 7 February 1950 as 'Associate States within the French Union'.[10] They would, it was then hoped, acquire greater independence (the French Union was much more tightly centralised than the British Commonwealth) and provide a focus for non-Communist nationalist aspirations. Neither hope seemed much nearer realisation in June 1953.

On the 30th of that month, for instance, Micky Joy, the Chargé d'Affaires in Saigon, dismissed the prospect that a political settlement might allow those nationalist leaders favoured by the French to compete for popular support with any hope of success: 'almost any terms would result, in a short space of time, in Communist control of Indochina, just as inevitably as would a Vietminh victory through French defection'.[11]

It was primarily because of Malaya that the French had to be pushed into effective measures to prevent Communist control of Indochina. Since 1948 a few thousand Communist guerrillas (about 5500 in 1953), whose Chinese race deprived them of support from the Malay majority, had been tying down a larger number of British troops and other forces in seemingly interminable jungle warfare. This they had done with no secure base, no reliable line of communications to a friendly frontier and depending on smugglers for a trickle of arms and ammunition. Macdonald's fear that Communist success in Indochina would produce a new government in Bangkok, anxious to conciliate their victorious Communist neighbours by tolerating an increased flow of the arms that would then be more readily available, was widely shared. In January 1953, for instance, the Defence Committee of the British Cabinet had decided that, if Siam were to succumb to Communism after a Vietminh conquest of Tonkin, British troops should enter Siam in strength and occupy the Songhkla position at a narrow stretch of the Kra isthmus north of the Malayan border. The military and political objections were acknowledged, but the Committee thought this might be the only way to save Malaya.[12]

It was scarcely surprising, therefore, that the Colonial Secretary (Oliver Lyttelton) warned the Cabinet on 6 July: 'it should not be assumed that, if the whole of Indochina came under Communist control, we should be able to prevent a deterioration of the situation in Malaya'.[13] On the following day his minute to Salisbury was more emphatic: 'it is thus vital to the security of Malaya that the French should achieve victory in Indochina'.[14]

The Cabinet had approved Lyttelton's proposal that the United States Government should be urged to give further assistance to the French in Indochina and Lyttelton as well as Selwyn Lloyd had endorsed the earlier Foreign Office brief on persuading the French to change their policies. These decisions, so carefully prepared and considered, nevertheless resulted in no substantial diplomatic representations, nor was Indochina again mentioned in Cabinet during 1953.

This inaction had various causes. The first was the disarray produced by Churchill's second and most serious stroke on 23 June 1953. Its gravity was not revealed to the public: the reference by his doctors to 'a disturbance of the cerebral circulation' was deleted from the communiqué issued on 27 June, which attributed to overwork his need for a complete rest.[15] But the Bermuda Conference, at which the French were to have been lectured, was indefinitely postponed and Churchill did not attend another Cabinet meeting until 18 August. R. A. Butler, the Chancellor of the Exchequer, presided in his place and Salisbury took over the Foreign Office.

On 30 June, admittedly, agreement was announced on a stop-gap meeting, to be held in Washington from 10 to 14 July, of the Foreign Ministers of Britain, France and the United States.

But Lord Salisbury, an able and intelligent man much liked in the Foreign Office for his business-like approach, the unassuming ease of his patrician manners and his lack of personal vanity or ambition, did not carry Churchill's weight as the bearer of unwelcome advice. Moreover, he had more important briefs to master for the Washington meeting and more urgent tasks to discharge when he got there. It is often forgotten how low Indochina ranked in the list of British priorities, Malaya notwithstanding, during the second half of 1953. Relations with the Soviet Union, the future of Germany and Austria, European defence: these were the giant problems. Even the unfinished business of the Korean War (the armistice was not signed until 27 July) outranked Indochina and Egypt was not merely high on the British agenda for Washington, but was the single aspect of foreign affairs most often and most extensively discussed by the British Cabinet during the second half of 1953.

Besides, the disagreeable and, as even Denis Allen had admitted in a minute of 7 July, probably hopeless task[16] of exhorting the French to greater efforts on this secondary issue seemed to have been pre-empted by the Laniel Government. On 3 July they had informed the governments of Cambodia, Laos and Vietnam of French determination to complete the sovereignty and independence of the Associated States by negotiating with each government a transfer of the powers hitherto reserved by France and a new definition of the links between these states and France. Admittedly the French announcement had attracted from Reggie Burrows, who looked after the affairs of Indochina in the South East Asia Department of the Foreign Office, the sour comment that 'it amounts to little more than a declaration that France will now, in 1953, implement the 1949 agreements'. His view was reflected in a supplementary brief for Washington[17] and would later be reinforced by a report from Micky Joy in Saigon that the French declaration had failed to make much impact on public opinion in Indochina.[18] But, if the Foreign Office had told Salisbury that the French declaration was inadequate, they had offered no detailed suggestions for its improvement. Even Macdonald, when holding out the unconditional grant of independence to India as a model, had proposed that such an offer should take effect in Indochina only after the war.

It is easy to argue that, over the years, the French had made the same mistake as the Dutch in Indonesia: not only always offering too little, too late; but proceeding piecemeal and hedging every advance with conditions and qualifications; never risking the single sweeping concession, the grand and reckless gesture capable of swaying popular emotions and converting Asian leaders. It is much harder to imagine what Salisbury could usefully have suggested to Bidault when they discussed Indochina on 13 July 1953.

Bidault had in any case taken the initiative. Georges Bidault, then aged 54, was already a statesman of impressively varied experience. Jesuit-educated, he had been a history teacher before the Second World War and a soldier (it will be important, in the course of our story, to note which of the principal figures had any personal knowledge of the nature of war) until France capitulated. Thereafter he had joined the Resistance, rose to lead its National Council in 1943 and, in that capacity, received General de Gaulle on his entry to Paris in 1944. These credentials and his real personal ability ensured him an outstanding political career. From 1944 to 1953 he was repeatedly in and out of government, as Prime Minister, Foreign Minister or Minister of Defence. In 1946 his decisions had played their part in launching the Indochina conflict and in June 1953 he had failed by one vote to become Prime Minister for the third time, perhaps because of his insistence on the power to rule by decree, perhaps because of his avowed determination to continue the struggle in Indochina. Now, for the fourth time, this intensely patriotic Frenchman, intelligent, fluent, capable of recklessness, already showing the physical and psychological lesions of an arduous career, but also a sophisticated politician, was French Foreign Minister.

He disconcerted both Dulles and Salisbury by telling them something they should have known, but had not expected to hear from him. 'It would not be possible for French opinion to accept a situation in which there was an armistice in Korea and a continuance of the war in Indochina.' He suggested that the political conference (it was envisaged by Article 4 of the Armistice, even if this had not yet been signed) should also take up the question of the situation in Indochina. Both Dulles and Salisbury were reserved, non-committal and somewhat discouraging in their responses, but Dulles told Salisbury privately that he was 'greatly surprised and disturbed by this development.' The Foreign Office, in response to Salisbury's request for comments, could only telegraph despondently: 'the

French attitude to Indochina is even more defeatist than expected'.[19]

Bidault also managed to block the second, military, pincer of the two-pronged assault which the Foreign Office had hoped Salisbury would launch against the French. The French Government, Bidault said, had not yet reached a decision on the military plans submitted by their new Commander-in-Chief in Indochina, General Henri Navarre.

Both the Americans, to whom the Navarre plan had earlier been disclosed in outline, and the British, who had some inkling, took a hopeful view of the General's ideas, but, on 11 July the British Embassy in Paris were discouraging. The Minister had learned that the French Chief of Staff had recommended, as Navarre wanted, the despatch of French conscripts to Indochina, but that there was little prospect of the Government agreeing and none of the National Assembly passing the necessary enabling legislation. Brigadier Macnab, the well-informed Military Attaché, was even blunter: no decisions are going to be taken in a hurry; no reinforcements are going to be sent out in a hurry; the war is *not* going to be won by the end of the year or by the end of next year either; no solution can be achieved by military means alone.[20]

As usual, the Embassy were broadly correct. The essence of the Navarre Plan was to create a mobile reserve able to operate offensively. Redispositions in Indochina apart, this required the despatch of reinforcements from Europe: ten to twelve of the French infantry battalions then committed to NATO. Navarre also wanted many additional French officers and NCOs so that he could use them as cadres to build up the strength of Vietnamese forces to a level that would allow a progressive withdrawal of French Union forces to begin in 18 months time.[21]

His plan was eventually approved, so the Embassy reported (optimistically) on 30 July, by the Committee of National Defence headed by President Auriol, but the nine battalions (none of them French), the 250 officers and 800 NCOs he was allegedly promised for 1954 were much less and later than he had wanted. Although Navarre himself always struck a confident note in public statements (if the Associated States really applied themselves to the war, 'la victoire est certaine') Brigadier Macnab commented on 31 July that Navarre had no hope of winning the war, merely of holding on until the Vietnamese could take over.[22]

By the end of July 1953, therefore, the French had offered
political concessions to the Associated States; these had been
welcomed by Dulles and Salisbury in the communiqué issued on
14 July after the Washington meeting; a plan had been approved
for a reinforced and more offensively minded military effort. The
French had done, of their own accord, what the British wanted.
Few supposed it would be enough.

As early as 14 July the Ambassador in Paris reported
complaints from one of Laniel's junior ministers (who had
himself visited Indochina) that French officials there were not
implementing the government's policy of greater independence
for the Associated States.[23] On the same date Mendès France
privately predicted a military débâcle in October. Micky Joy,
criticising the calibre of French representatives in Indochina,
remarked on their inability 'to disguise their contempt for the
inhabitants'.[24] The British Consul in Hanoi described the low
morale of both the French and their Vietnamese auxiliaries in the
critical northern sector, the Red River Delta.[25]

As August wore on into September, Joy's reports of the
difficulties being experienced by the French in their attempts to
reach a political understanding with the Cambodian and
Vietnamese governments (only in Laos were negotiations going
smoothly) were not balanced by any note of encouragement in the
regular reports from his Military Attaché. Neither situation was
dramatically worse – the tone of the Saigon Summary for August
was typical: 'in Cambodia the security situation has continued to
degenerate slowly'[26] – but the improvement everyone was hoping
for had yet to materialise. There was no crisis, no new reason for
the tocsin sounded, with such effort and so little result, at the end
of June. Such attention, moreover, as Ministers and their senior
advisers could spare for Indochina was focused on a different
aspect: Bidault's suggestion for negotiations.

It was 1 August before a call from the French Ambassador in
London, Massigli, clarified the purport of the obscure
memorandum (the Foreign Office could not even make out
whether a reply was expected) Bidault had himself circulated.
The first object of the French Government was to obtain a
cessation of Chinese logistic help to the Vietminh, this to be
followed by a cease-fire. Thereafter it might be possible to open
talks with the Chinese. The French accordingly wanted to know
how the problem of Indochina could be brought within the

general ambit of the Political Conference on Korea (a conference, incidentally, which had yet to be arranged). The United States Government did not want the question to be put on the agenda, so the French wondered whether a parallel conference might be a possibility.

Salisbury was dubious about a parallel conference, but said that Her Majesty's Government 'would certainly not oppose consideration of the Indochina problem at a Korean Conference'.[27] This reasonable reply (it was, after all, a *French* problem) caused a continuing bureaucratic fuss because different language had been used by the Americans and by Selwyn Lloyd, until Salisbury put his foot down on 27 September: 'I hold strongly to the view that Indochina ought to come second on the list for the Political Conference'.[28] Nobody, however, produced any constructive ideas for initiating such negotiations and it was Laniel, on 10 September, who hit on what would eventually prove the way forward, when he suggested that the projected Four Power meeting on the German question might provide a framework for the settlement of wider problems, including the restoration of peace in Indochina.[29]

The low priority accorded to Indochina in Whitehall during the third quarter of 1953 reflected British public opinion. The only discussion in the House of Commons was on 21 July, when Attlee, Leader of the Opposition, endorsed the Government view that 'a successful outcome of this struggle is a matter of the utmost concern', but the more left-wing Ian Mikardo insisted, in presumably unconscious echo of the Foreign Office, that we were backing a loser in the French. But there was no passion in the brief discussion, not a flicker of the emotional response Indochina would evoke in Britain a dozen years later.[30] The *New Statesman*'s comment – 'British foreign policy is back in the Foreign Office pigeon-hole . . . a fight to the finish in Indochina' – was a mere reflex response.[31]

The Times relied on its Paris correspondent as the source of news on Indochina and seldom allowed his regular reports to stray beyond the page then headed 'Imperial and Foreign'. There was only one leading article of any note – on 29 August. This called Bao Dai (presumably the writer had once talked to His Imperial Majesty's principal admirer – Malcolm Macdonald) 'a figure of significance' to Western hopes that the national movement in

Indochina could be prevented from becoming a Communist monopoly. It was not otherwise an optimistic article.

Bao Dai was more remarkable than significant. Hereditary emperor of Annam, one of the three constituent parts of Vietnam, he had abdicated in 1945 to become 'supreme adviser' to Ho Chi Minh, but abandoned him to form new ideas in Hong Kong in 1946. Subsequently recruited by the French, he had signed the 1949 agreement establishing the notional independence of Vietnam and was recognised as its Head of State. As such he was often a source of embarrassment, but he sensibly preferred the pursuit of pleasure to that of power and spent much of his time at Cannes. The Military Attaché in Saigon, perhaps unduly influenced by Bao Dai's arriving 50 minutes late for a passing-out parade of Vietnamese officers, had dismissed him on 1 July as 'a very sick man – fat and bloated'.[32] He was more than that and he often meant well, but, as the figurehead of Vietnamese nationalism, he could not win.

British indifference was naturally not echoed in France, where, as the Embassy repeatedly reported, the attention of ministers and politicians was focused on Indochina, even if the public mood, in the words of *The Times* correspondent, was one of 'distaste and weariness' for the war.[33]. Nor was there any apathy in the United States, whose rulers were preoccupied by French demands for additional financial assistance and warnings that refusal would lead to the fall of the Laniel government and its replacement by one bent on withdrawal from Indochina. These tactics resulted in a joint Franco-American communiqué on 30 September announcing an American contribution of $385 million in 1954 to finance (it was subsequently estimated) two thirds of that year's French military expenditure in Indochina, together with a French undertaking 'à faire tous ses efforts pour disloquer et détruire les forces régulières de l'ennemi en Indochine'.[34] This promise to fight on was, as the British Embassy later reported, received with little enthusiasm in France.[35]

In Indochina men of numerous nationalities, together with too many women and children, continued to be killed. King Norodom Sihanouk of Cambodia was displaying a patriotic fervour in his intransigent negotiations with the French that embarrassed even American advocates of indigenous nationalism and, on 17 September, Bao Dai published an imperial decree that would have unexpected consequences. Two hundred hand-picked Vietnamese, supposedly representative of all the acceptable strands of public opinion, were to be chosen as members of a National Congress. This would meet for two days, at a date to be appointed, to advise the Vietnamese Government on two aspects of the negotiations proposed by the Laniel Government on 3 July: the nature and extent of Vietnamese national sovereignty and future links with France.[36]

Ostensibly the British prescription for the ills of Indochina was being followed, as usually happens, as far as would cause no inconvenience to the patients, who preserved the customary reticence about the gravity of their symptoms and the laxity of their régime.

2   Waiting upon Events

'We do not want to be alarmist, but we must be alert to the possibility of seriously adverse developments as the current campaign develops.'—JOHN TAHOURDIN[1]

On 8 September 1953, Mr Ogburn, the Regional Planning Adviser in the State Department's Bureau of Far Eastern Affairs, concluded a wide-ranging memorandum on Alternatives in Indochina with the words:

'So far our policy on Indochina has been based on an article of faith which has been considered not subject to question: the French cannot and must not fail. With evidence accumulating, however, that the French can and may fail, is not the time at hand when we ought to consider what we can do in anticipation of such a failure?'

There were no Planners then in the Foreign Office, but anyone asking such an awkward question would probably have received much the same reply as Mr Ogburn, whose superior told him the next day: 'We must not *let* the Navarre Plan fail'.[2] In London the Chiefs of Staff discussed a paper by the Joint Intelligence Committee on Future Developments in Indochina and their Consequences Elsewhere. The record of their discussion is closed to the public for 50 years, but it is not hard to guess its tenor. Neither politically nor militarily were the French acting as decisively as British experts thought they should, but at least the French had taken a step in the right direction and should be given a chance. That was on 28 September[3] and the Chiefs of Staff did not again discuss Indochina until 5 November, when they poured cold water on French fears of military intervention by aircraft based in China.[4]

The Foreign Office were no more active and 1953 expired without any renewal, except at the lowest level, of the major effort made in June to alert Ministers to the menacing problems of

Indochina and to the consequential need to reconsider the assumptions and objectives of British policy.

During these months, of course, there was the usual evolution, biological rather than rational, of the accepted concepts of that policy. Malcolm Macdonald, always an optimist, had nevertheless been the first to suggest the shift of emphasis. In a telegram of 21 July he argued that the new French measures, if fully implemented, should enable them to establish a strong military ascendancy in about 18 months and then to negotiate, either with non-communist nationalists or with non-communist elements in the Vietminh, from a position of strength.[5] Although non-communists were not the people who could negotiate an end to the war and were not so regarded by the French, the slogan of 'negotiating from strength' caught on. From an aspiration it became a caveat – negotiations should *only* take place from a position of strength – the stock formula used in briefing Ministers as late as 10 December.[6] By then it was becoming painfully obvious that any position of strength was unlikely to be a French achievement.

Obvious, that is, to some of the British officials involved. All through the last quarter of 1953 discouragement flowed from Paris and Saigon. At the beginning of October the Embassy reported the hostile reaction of the French press to the communiqué announcing $385 million of American aid for the Indochina war,[7] even though Jacquet, the junior minister responsible for the Associated States, had earlier declared, with calculated ambiguity, 'l'aide américain supplémentaire n'a pas pour but de "nourrir" la guerre en Indochine, mais de la terminer'.[8]

On 17 October the Embassy reported 'consternation' because the supposedly docile Vietnamese National Congress (organised, as mentioned in the previous chapter, by Bao Dai) had resolved that 'independent Vietnam will not adhere to the French Union in its present form'.[9] That sober publication (the equivalent of the *Annual Register*) *L'Année Politique 1953* subsequently recorded that this resolution deprived years of French sacrifices in Indochina of all their meaning[10] and Bidault told Eden and Dulles at a Tripartite Meeting in London the same day that this would make it hard to convince French opinion of the need to continue the war effort. Nevertheless, Bidault insisted, General Navarre had created his mobile reserve and reinforcements would reach him by the end of the month. Eden wished the French every success and the communiqué said a successful conclusion of the war was 'an essential step towards the re-establishment of peace in Asia'.[11] The Paris Embassy, however, soon reported that the Laniel Government had only survived a long and critical debate in the National Assembly by introducing a resolution implying that the Vietnamese would themselves increasingly assume the burden of the war yet agree to remain in the French Union.[12]

The Economist summed it up neatly on 7 November: 'the French are not prepared to engage in the fight against Communism just for its own sake. In the past, Frenchmen have regarded the war in Indochina as a purely patriotic effort in defence of what were at first regarded as vital French interests. But now the game no longer seems worth the candle.'

The Times chose, as we shall see, a peculiarly appropriate date for its leader of Friday 13 November expressing confidence in the Navarre Plan and declaring that the war could only be lost in Paris. The half-truth in that argument, popular in military circles then and later, needs to be qualified by the reports reaching the Foreign Office from Saigon. The Military Attaché (there were two of them, Brigadier T. H. Spear and Major A. G. Graham, but the former admitted that their extensive travels made it difficult to assign individual responsibility for their reporting) was seldom optimistic. A significant report on 3 November described the arrival of the smart French battalion hitherto employed in Korea: 'the first time I have seen a battalion of white or nearly white troops since I arrived here – in fact it is the only one in Indochina'.[13]

What he did not report was the arrival of any other battalions. Even now much work is required from some military historian to rescue the full truth about those reinforcements from the mist of ambiguity in which French writers have left it: between, that is, the two clear landmarks represented by successive decisions of the Committee of National Defence under President Auriol. On 24 July 1953, the Committee approved the Navarre Plan in principle, but made no precise commitment about reinforcements;[14] on that 13 November which had ironically inspired *The Times* the Committee decided that the resources of the French Union were already fully stretched in Europe and North Africa (there had been trouble in Morocco and Tunisia) and that the forces at Navarre's disposal could not be further increased.[15]

What seems to have happened in between is that North African and African units were sent to Indochina, but, as Navarre had feared would be the case, partly as reliefs rather than as net reinforcements.[16] For the purposes of our story it is enough to note that between 1 July 1953 and 1 January 1954 the strength of French Union land forces in Indochina (French, Foreign Legion, North African and African) increased by 4815 officers and men, nearly 4 per cent or, allowing for the inclusion in these figures of other arms, the equivalent of four or five infantry battalions. If one adds in air force, navy, women and Indochinese soldiers in the French Union forces, the total increase was under 4000 or 2 per cent. Within these totals the numbers of French and Foreign Legion soldiers actually declined.[17]

Remembering that the British Chiefs of Staff had assessed the reinforcements required at two to three divisions and that Navarre had originally asked for ten to twelve battalions of *French* soldiers, it is clear that one of the fundamental conditions of the Navarre Plan – significant reinforcement – had not been met and that the optimistic impression conveyed by Bidault to his American and British colleagues on 17 October had been somewhat misleading.

There is no evidence in the surviving papers in the Public Record Office – from which, admittedly, much has been withheld on dubious pretexts of continuing secrecy – that this basic flaw in American, British, even French assumptions about the likelihood of reaching a position of strength in Indochina was ever appreciated in London. Even when Sir Oliver Harvey, taking advantage of Eden's presence in Paris on 16 December 1953 and clearly believing that Bidault's misleading optimism at Bermuda about the French military position in Indochina had not been adequately corrected, asked Eden to read a minute by the Military Attaché, this did not even mention the reinforcement issue. Brigadier Macnab's forecast, gloomy as ever, was based on the evident unfitness of Vietnamese troops to replace French Union forces in static defence and thus allow Navarre to regroup and prepare for offensive operations.[18]

Admittedly, the Military Attachés in both Paris and Saigon were heavily dependent on the French for their information, but this did not prevent either from trying to ferret out the facts or from expressing views at variance with French briefing. On 8 November, for instance, General Navarre, announcing the conclusion of the first stage of his campaign to regain the initiative, Operation MOUETTE, had declared 'I am now confident of success.' On the 10th Brigadier Spear, while conceding that the operation had not been defeated, thought it had failed to achieve the objective intended.

> The state of the Delta itself is certainly no better than it was last year. In fact . . . it is worse and the Vietminh hold of it is stronger than ever.
> The French/Vietnamese forces are in for a very hard time this winter . . . they will pull through . . . but they may take some heavy punishment . . . and this will have a serious effect on public opinion not only in France and America but also in this country [Indochina].

It was unfortunate that this report, and its well-founded predictions, achieved no further penetration in the Foreign Office than the Assistant in South East Asia Department. Military writing is admittedly prolix, but many of the Military Attaché's lengthy reports should have been briefly summarised for higher authority.[19]

Ministers, of course, continued to be preoccupied by the different problems mentioned in the previous chapter. These were augmented by the first Soviet test, on 12 August, of a hydrogen bomb, by growing concern at French reluctance to ratify the treaties establishing the European Defence Community, by a new crisis over Trieste and, throughout the second half of 1953, by the elephantine minuet in which the Soviet Union, Britain, France and the still rather nebulous plans for the political conference conditions for a conference of the four powers on the problems of Central Europe. Even Denis Allen (responsible, of course, for the whole of Asia) was kept busy by the aftermath of the Korean War and the still rather nebulous plans for the politial conference envisaged by the Armistice Agreement of 27 July 1953.

There were also preoccupations of a more domestic, even personal character. On 1 October 1953 Anthony Eden returned from the long convalescence that had followed his illness and his three major operations. He had, of course, endeavoured to keep in touch with the political scene at home and abroad – it was the all-absorbing interest of his life – during the six months he had been away. Nevertheless his interview that morning with the

Prime Minister came as something of a shock. Churchill was clearly determined to carry on. Eden was neither offered a new post to prepare him for the succession nor satisfied by the old man's promise to quit if he found he could not 'fully do his duty'.[20]

Churchill's attitude was cause enough for legitimate concern and worried many cabinet ministers. His doctor, Lord Moran, had recorded his own view as early as 3 July:

> He will never again be the same man as he was before the stroke, because the clot in his artery has cut off some of the blood which went to his brain and was the ultimate source of all his activities. So his brain is always anaemic, and when the circulation flags a little, then he has no zest for work and cannot face detail . . . he is really living on a volcano and he may get another stroke at any time.[21]

Though largely borne out by events, this depressing prognosis was incomplete. Churchill did have his bad days, was easily tired even on his good and was often regarded by colleagues and staff as unfit for his job. But he still had ideas and could express them forcibly. His instincts tended to be sounder than the judgment and discrimination, always weak points, he brought to their pursuit. He retained his authority as often as he had the energy to exert it. With his immense prestige he was a difficult man to dislodge as long as he wanted to stay.

And he did. Not only because the exercise of power was the breath of his life, but because, deeply disturbed by Soviet acquisition of the hydrogen bomb, he was more than ever determined on one final achievement: laying the foundations of a lasting peace at a Summit Conference with the Russians. This ambition was distressing to his colleagues, who feared Churchill might alienate the Americans only to be rebuffed by the Russians. They were also sceptical of useful results and sure Churchill was not fit for such negotiations.

These responsible apprehensions, this patriotic wish to see Churchill relinquish responsibilities he was no longer fully capable of discharging, were aggravated in Eden's case by acute anxiety about the succession. Since at least 1951 Eden had expected to step into Churchill's shoes and his hopes had been encouraged, not only by Churchill himself, but by influential members of the Conservative Party. Naturally he also had rivals and critics, whose influence and intrigues were always exaggerated by his anxious temperament. Eden's long illness had not only given Churchill a fresh excuse for postponing his own retirement but had provided Eden's opponents, real or imagined, with a new argument. In politics timing is as important as the mood of the moment and Eden not only wanted Churchill to go, but was acutely conscious of the need to keep his own reputation burnished. When the opportunity he so longed for finally came, he had to be ready to step forward in the shining armour of success.

These were important considerations for a man so ambitious, so sensitive, so lonely and so insecure as Eden. Anthony Nutting, then Parliamentary Under Secretary in the Foreign Office, described Eden – and the description has been endorsed by others who worked closely with him at the time – as 'essentially more vain than most politicians'.[22] Evelyn Shuckburgh, his Principal Private Secretary, commented in his contemporary diary that Eden 'is like a sea anemone, covered with sensitive tentacles all recording currents of opinion around him. He quivers with sensitivity to opinion in the House, the party, the newspapers'.[23] This acute self-consciousness was allied to a jealous disposition and was sometimes vented in sulks, petulance, bursts of irritation and even an outright rudeness that contrasted strangely with the charm he could so well display when he wished and for which he was famous.

Naturally this temperamental instability affected his conduct of affairs and instances will appear in subsequent chapters. Its influence should not be exaggerated. Eden was deeply patriotic (a distinguished soldier in the war of 1914–18) as well as intensely ambitious. His experience in foreign affairs, before, during and after the Second World War, surpassed that of any of the principal actors in this drama, an asset he did not always conceal from them. Even those officials who suffered from his foibles (and not all of them did) admitted he knew the work of the Office as well as they did themselves. He was a good diplomat and a skilful negotiator. Once involved in the affairs of Indochina his instincts were usually sound even if he sometimes lacked the courage of his convictions and was often a prey to indecision.

In the autumn of 1953, however, he had much else on his mind. Both he and Salisbury spoke about foreign policy at the Conservative Party Conference (8–10 October). Egypt ranked as high as any of the world's major problems. Korea was mentioned, but not Indochina.[24]

Indochina nevertheless came to his notice on 5 October 1953 (the day he resumed, rather reluctantly and against medical advice, charge of the Foreign Office). He then warned Casey, the Australian Minister for External Affairs, that there were 'grave dangers' in the idea, which Casey attributed to Dulles, of using Kuomintang troops from Formosa to help the French in Indochina.[25] This may have been in Eden's mind when he circulated, on 24 November, a Cabinet Paper on Policy in the Far East, the only one on this subject in 1953. Eden argued that the Communist threat was now most active in Asia and spoke of 'broad agreement with the United States Government that Communism must be contained in the Far East.' Differences with the Americans were over methods, the choice of friends and machinery. Without going into detail and revealing no special sense of urgency, the paper foreshadowed many of the divergences that would become acute in 1954. A key sentence was: 'The United States Administration find it difficult to pursue a realistic policy towards China.'[26]

They did, indeed, the ruling Republicans having made China the partisan shibboleth of American politics. Red China, as it was always described to distinguish it from the Republic of China in Formosa, was regarded with a religious horror different in kind from the more rational fear and hostility excited by the Soviet Union, even though both countries were supposed to belong to a monolithic Sino-Soviet bloc directed from Moscow. Dulles might privately concede, at the Bermuda Conference in December, that Mao's prestige would probably compel Malenkov (then the Soviet leader) to treat him as an equal partner, but this was no mitigation of Mao's communism.[27] And behind the doctrinaire Dulles, that 'curious cross between a Christer and a shrewd and quite ruthless lawyer', as one of his biographers described him,[28] were fanatics still more extreme, intent on keeping him up to their intransigent standards of anti-Communist purity. One of them was Senator Joseph R. McCarthy, whose witch-hunt was regularly and censoriously reported in the British press and whose henchman McLeod (appointed by Dulles to head the Bureau of Security and Personnel) was then conducting a reign of terror in the State Department 'immolating on the way the careers of several hundred officers and employees',[29] including a number previously concerned with Chinese affairs.

Other governments might be less excitable about China

without being much more knowledgeable. The French, from understandable motives of national pride, tended to exaggerate both Chinese responsibility for the insurrection in Indochina and the dependence of the Vietminh on Chinese military assistance. They also hoped the Chinese might somehow be persuaded to save France from the humiliation of negotiating with Ho Chi Minh. Mendès France had ridiculed this idea as early as 28 May 1953,[30] but Bidault continued to hanker after it. Even when he conceded, at Bermuda on 7 December, that China would certainly not admit any responsibility,[31] his advocacy of a Five Power Conference seems to have reflected the hope that Chinese good-will might be forthcoming as the price of her admission to international society, a view, without its specifically Indochinese slant, that found echoes in London.

French hopes initially received little Chinese encouragement. On 8 October, when Chou en Lai, the Chinese Prime Minister, formally endorsed the Soviet proposal of 28 September 'for the convening of a Conference of Foreign Ministers of the Five Great Powers ... to examine measures for the relaxation of international tension', Indochina was not among the problems mentioned in his long and repetitive statement.[32] Instead the first significant move came from Ho Chi Minh whose announcement was published by the Swedish newspaper *Expressen* on 29 November:

'If the French Government wish to have an armistice and to resolve the question of Vietnam by means of negotiations, the people and government of the Democratic Republic of Vietnam are ready to examine the French proposals.[33]

His statement naturally received the support of the Chinese and Soviet governments and must, British officials agreed at the time, have been cleared with them in advance,[34] but Ho Chi Minh was not the leader from whom French ministers most hoped to hear such words.

The impact in France was nevertheless considerable. Laniel had hitherto been able to take the line, notably on 12 November, that his expressed readiness for negotiations – 'une solution honorable ... une solution diplomatique du conflit' – had attracted no response from the other side.[35] This defence had now disappeared, though Laniel could still argue that Ho Chi Minh's proposal was unacceptable, because it ignored the existence of the Associated States as parties to the conflict, a point noted with dismay in Indochina. On 1 December, however, *The Times* reported that the desire in Paris for an end to hostilities was so strong that no French government could afford not to explore the Vietminh proposal.

Laniel did his best, telling the US Chargé d'Affaires on 30 November that the statement would not alter French policy – certainly not pending full consultation at the forthcoming Bermuda Conference.[36]

The Summit Meeting of Churchill, Eisenhower and Laniel, which took place at Bermuda in the first week of December 1953, had again been arranged at Churchill's insistence. Eisenhower was a reluctant participant and the French came with mixed feelings, anxious to be present but aware they would be exposed to pressure. Churchill was the first to arrive on 2 December, looking, as *The Times* reported, 'pale and bent' after a rough journey, but pleased to be met by a guard of honour of the Royal Welch Fusiliers with the regimental goat, an animal whose diplomatic importance had been somewhat misjudged. Of course the French might not have resented Churchill's turning his back on Laniel to caress the goat, if only the band had earlier played the Marseillaise, an unfortunate omission from the pageantry of military welcome to which the Prime Minister had given his personal attention well in advance.[37]

This could scarcely be said of his numerous official briefs. These covered a wide range of contentious issues, Indochina ranking low and sufficiently summarised in a minute by Reggie Burrows: French embarrassment at Ho Chi Minh's statement notwithstanding, 'negotiations should only take place from a position of strength'.[38] Shuckburgh did not even mention Indochina in his diary (or ever in 1953) when commenting on the following day's discussion between Churchill and his principal advisers. The Prime Minister had been 'confused and wrong on every issue . . . raring to be rude to the French . . . old, weary and inconsequent'.

Churchill's ill temper, emphasised by Moran in his own journal,[39] was sustained and seemed infectious. Only Laniel, who took to his bed with pneumonia soon after his arrival, escaped. On 4 December Shuckburgh found Eisenhower 'very rude I thought and vulgar'. Eden was alarmed by the apparent readiness of the Americans to contemplate the use of nuclear weapons and Shuckburgh surprised by the 'strangely wild and distraught look' in Eisenhower's eyes, not when speaking himself, but while listening. Bidault, in Laniel's absence, took most of the strain – on 6 December – 'very bad atmosphere with the French in the dock.' The next day, Shuckburgh recorded: 'everybody very angry, appeals, sentiment, Bidault looks like a dying man, Laniel is actually dying upstairs. . . . Outburst by Eisenhower and Winston, former left the conference table in a rage, came back, having changed for dinner, sat another 4 hours'.[40]

Curously enough, in view of later events, the easiest relationship in this indecorous conference was that between Eden and Dulles. They lay amicably together on the beach, Eden soaking up the sun and Dulles displaying some gaudy shorts that belied his reputation for puritan austerity ('This fellow preaches like a Methodist Minister' Churchill had complained).[41] Both, but particularly Eden, had to work very hard indeed to get an agreed communiqué on the last night, even invading the sick-room of poor, fever-tossed Laniel in their efforts.

Although unanimity on any subject scarcely existed, the issue that most excited these angry old men was French reluctance to ratify the European Defence Community. An earlier French government had once hoped this contrivance might make German rearmament more palatable to French opinion. So many Frenchmen had since decided it tasted worse than the nasty medicine itself that parliamentary ratification had never been attempted. HM Embassy at Paris had reported that voting in November's long foreign affairs debate in the National Assembly showed a majority against it,[42] but the British and American intention at Bermuda was to push the Laniel Government into the effort. The US Government had earlier had to be dissuaded by their Ambassador in Paris from making aid to Indochina conditional on French ratification[43] and the Chargé d'Affaires in Saigon was later told to deny the rumoured existence of such a condition.[44]

When given the chance at Bermuda to talk about Indochina, the French, ritual optimism about the military situation apart, had concentrated on negotiations. Before his pneumonia took hold, Laniel told the Americans he wanted first to establish a position of military strength, but that President Auriol and others wanted immediate negotiations.[45] Bidault maintained his personal preference for continuing the struggle, but described French public opinion as 'indifferent or weary' and insisted that 'the French people should not be faced with an unending dreary plain of continued war' now that there was an armistice in Korea.[46] He said his government's response to Ho Chi Minh's proposals had been intended to exclude bilateral talks and that a Five Power Conference might be the solution provided the Associated States were represented.[47]

Eisenhower retorted that a Five Power Conference was 'a bad word for the United States',[48] but neither his offer of more aid nor Churchill's allusion to the example set by the British in Malaya were politically relevant in France. Even Bidault's rejection of bilateral talks did not, as both the Foreign Office and the Paris Embassy soon pointed out,[49] command the full support of the French government or people. The only concrete achievement of the Bermuda Conference – its expression of readiness for a Four Power Meeting of Foreign Ministers with the Russians – would, as Burrows predicted on 9 December,[50] encourage Bidault to take this fresh opportunity of suggesting a Five Power Conference.

The stories that leaked from the Bermuda Conference (that object lesson to those who call for summit meetings in the cause of international harmony) also aroused, as both the Embassy and *L'Année Politique* reported,[51] a sense of grievance in France, though more against the British than the Americans. Bidault himself denied that he had been ill-treated, but such sentiments did not make it any easier for him to achieve in Paris the agreement on policy towards Indochina that had eluded him in Bermuda. The differences of French Ministers were those of hope rather than rational expectation. A negotiated end to the war was the common denominator imposed by public opinion, but how, when and on what terms? Most probably looked either to General Navarre or to some understanding among the Great Powers to provide the essential preliminary: some strengthening of France's bargaining position. Readiness to wait for the right moment, however, was diminishing.

The chances of this difficult problem receiving patient and concentrated analysis were further hampered by two distractions. Dulles had gone on the rampage, distressing public opinion in Britain as well as France, by threatening an 'agonising reappraisal' of the entire policy of the United States if France failed to ratify the treaties establishing the European Defence Community.[52] And the two most resolute members of the French Government, Laniel and Bidault, were both candidates to succeed Auriol as President of France. Bidault dropped out after two ballots, but Laniel persisted for ten, René Coty finally being elected on 23 December after 13 ballots in seven days. As *L'Année Politique* described the month of December: 'L'expiration des pouvoirs de M. Auriol approchant, les réunions gouvernementales se font moins nombreuses.'[53]

Also on 23 December Vice-President Nixon, who had recently visited Indochina, told the National Security Council in Washington: 'I am convinced that negotiation at the present time would be disastrous.'[54]

In London Reggie Burrows, then the only Foreign Office official solely concerned with Indochina, wrote a long minute on 18 December. 'In the near future', he began, 'the French Government may actively be seeking to end the Indochina war.' He concluded that the time had come to consider the possible alternatives if present British policy could no longer be continued: direct negotiations between France and the Vietminh; inclusion of Indochina in a general settlement at which the Associated States would be represented; replacement of the French in Indochina by the Americans or reference of the Indochina situation to the United Nations. This prescient minute attracted various comments from other departments, but had made no progress upwards by the end of the year.[55]

In Saigon attention was on Dien Bien Phu. On 24 November the Military Attaché reported its encouraging seizure by a spectacular French airborne attack. On 15 December he wondered, but was still optimistic: 'will it be tenable once the landing ground comes under effective observed artillery fire?' On 29 December (the Military Attaché's report had come by bag) Burrows, who had himself been a pilot employed in the precarious airborne support of similarly beleaguered Imphal in 1944, minuted that Dien Bien Phu might develop into the big fight of the season. Whichever way the Vietminh moved, their purpose would be to seek a spectacular success. For once this report and minute went up to Denis Allen.[56]

In fact the Vietminh had chosen a major raid into Laos, one of the options the hedgehog of Dien Bien Phu had been meant to block. The main headline in *The Times* of 28 December was INDOCHINA CUT IN TWO BY VIETMINH FORCES and the French press, the Embassy reported, were dismayed.[57] Saigon, however, telegraphed on 30 December that the raid was a propaganda stunt. 'Dien Bien Phu is a more important zone to watch. In a short time the enemy will have about 22 battalions with anti-aircraft support and some field artillery grouped around a defending force of about 10 battalions who already dispose of artillery and air support.'

General Navarre, the Paris Embassy reported, was 'supremely confident', but a further telegram from Saigon on 31 December said: 'possibility of all out attack on Dien Bien Phu now appears likely'.

'If it succeeded', Burrows minuted on 2 January 1954, 'and the large French garrison failed to hold, it would be a catastrophe for France. . . . I attach a draft self-contained minute for submission higher up if this is thought desirable.'

His minute reached the Head of South East Asia Department, whose comment is recorded at the head of this chapter.[58]

3   Changing Course

'It would be unrealistic not to face the possibility that the conditions for a favourable solution in Indochina may no longer exist.'—FOREIGN OFFICE TEL to Washington of 1 April 1954[1]

When 1954 began it was clear to dispassionate observers that French efforts to crush the Vietminh insurrection were destined to early failure. Dispassionate, however, was no word to use of the principal actors. For months to come Dulles, Malcolm Macdonald, intermittently even General Navarre would continue to express unreal hopes of eventual victory. Bidault remained schizophrenic to the end. Conscious, as a politician, that the French people would no longer support the war; he could not, as a patriot, consistently draw the logical conclusion. He was not alone, nor were his countrymen. The evidence that lends intellectual credibility to an unwelcome prediction is often insufficient to make it politically acceptable.

For those American and European officials knowledgeably interested in Indochina there was a twofold problem: how to explain that ultimate French success was no longer a valid assumption; and what substitute to propose for the previously accepted policy of, with a little British and much American logistic assistance, leaving Indochina to the French? In London, unlike Washington, this scarcely seemed an urgent task. Ministers still had other preoccupations and only the Third Room (the lowest level in the Foreign Office hierarchy) of the South East Asia Department wanted to disturb existing attitudes to Indochina. Perhaps this was because none of their seniors had served in South East Asia since the Second World War and thus took a more sanguine view of the prospects. To them it seemed that all that was needed was a routine brief for the quadripartite Berlin Conference of Foreign Ministers, in which Indochina seemed likely to surface as a peripheral issue.

On 15 January 1954 this brief recommended that Her

41

Majesty's Government should sustain the French Government in their present policy of refusing to negotiate an Indochina settlement except on conditions that would safeguard the independence of the Associated States.[2] This was, perhaps, a trifle concise at the end of a fortnight in which Dien Bien Phu had been encircled; in which Navarre had admitted to the United States Ambassador that it might fall;[3] in which Laniel had asked the United States for more bomber aircraft;[4] in which the National Security Council in Washington had discussed American intervention[5] and in which Dulles had warned China and Eisenhower had promised France another four hundred million dollars.[6]

These were details. What mattered was that the brief was a contradiction in terms. The independence of the Associated States was what the French had been fighting for years to safeguard. It was only because they were visibly failing, that anyone had ever considered negotiations. But the Vietminh were not going to concede at the conference table, let alone as a condition of sitting at that table, what they had successfully resisted on the battlefield.

Denis Allen, who must have approved the brief because he accompanied Eden to Berlin, knew that perfectly well. This quietly spoken New Zealander, then 44 years old, united a command of the facts with a gift for their exposition which had given him an influence over Eden usually enjoyed only by officials of more forceful and dominating personality. To his juniors he was always courteous, but a little remote, making it difficult to understand just why this able and intelligent man took a relatively optimistic view of the situation in Indochina.

The new formula was a more tactful and topical version of the previous month's 'negotiations can only take place usefully from a position of strength'.[7] The words had changed, but not the tune: the French had to be kept in the fight. Malcolm Macdonald thought another two years would see the establishment of a decisive French military ascendancy.[8]

The French themselves were not so sure. Before the Berlin Conference, which was supposed to be mainly about Germany, had even begun, Bidault urged Dulles in a private meeting of the three Western Ministers on 23 January 1954 to accept the principle of a Five Power Conference on Indochina. Dulles was non-commital, but insisted that China could not be accepted as one of 5 Great Powers. Eden, when alone with Nutting, the

Parliamentary Under-Secretary, and Evelyn Shuckburgh, was enthusiastic. In spite of their discouragement,[9] Eden got the Cabinet to endorse his view that it would be inexpedient to resist a proposal for a Five Power meeting confined to Far Eastern questions and beginning with Korea.[10] Although it took weeks to overcome the opposition of Dulles and to pin down the wavering Bidault, Eden's view eventually prevailed and on 18 February the Berlin Conference agreed 'that the problem of restoring peace in Indochina will also be discussed at the Conference [on the Korean question], to which representatives of the United States, France, the United Kingdom, the Union of Soviet Socialist Republics, and the Chinese People's Republic and other interested states will be invited'.[11]

Berlin was a more decorous conference than Bermuda, but it had its undercurrents. Bidault later recalled that Dulles had tried to please him by criticising Eden,[12] who was himself amused to be the recipient of Bidault's acid comments on Dulles.[13] The process of reaching agreement also had some peculiar features. Eden, so his Private Secretary thought, wanted a Five Power Conference as a personal 'success' to take home from what would otherwise be a fruitless meeting at Berlin.[14] Molotov, so Eden plausibly suggested,[15] wanted one to placate his increasingly restive Chinese allies. Dulles was adamant against any proposal to admit China to international society and feared the prospect of a Conference would undermine Navarre's offensive and incite the Vietminh to fresh efforts. He gave way only because this 'was made inescapable by pressure on Bidault.'[16]

He chose the right description. Bidault was under pressure from France. Margerie, his diplomatic adviser, had early told British and American officials that no French government could refuse a Five Power Conference which offered an honourable means of bringing the war in Indochina to an end. Bidault himself, as always, spent the Conference in two minds, sometimes urgent for negotiations, but also tempted by his dream of making China cease helping the Vietminh as the price of her own participation. Only at the last minute did he accept Molotov's formula and he could not bring himself to mention Indochina in his final speech. Eden, characteristically, was alone in welcoming the prospect of talks and looking forward 'to our meeting in Geneva.'[17] Only in Washington was the news received with actual sourness (though there seem to have been complaints in Peking that Molotov could have done more to establish China's equal status as a Great Power)[18] and both Eisenhower and Dulles had to justify themselves privately by arguing that continued American opposition would have brought down the only French government willing to attempt the defence of Indochina or the ratification of the European Defence Community.[19]

Eden, of course, had merely decided there should be a conference with Indochina on the agenda, but the name of Geneva now became a weapon in the hands of those members of the Third Room of the South East Asia Department who had long advocated reconsideration of British policy towards Indochina. My minute (I had taken over that week from Reggie Burrows, who was on leave before posting) of 23 February 1954[20] fell on less stony ground than his of 18 December 1953.[21] On 3 March I was even able to produce the first draft of a policy paper. Progress was slow and hard-fought, but by 1 April the paper had been cleared with other departments and with the Joint Intelligence Committee, endorsed by the Chiefs of Staff and approved by Eden.

The final version bore its bureaucratic scars. The old policy – keeping the French in the fight, negotiating only from strength – was restated at the outset and reiterated from time to time as a staunch refrain. Unfortunately, the paper lamented:

> the will to press on to a military victory has quite disappeared in France . . . militarily – the initiative remains with the Vietminh . . . any direct intervention by the armed forces of any external nation [Chinese nationalists had been considered as well as Americans] would probably result in Chinese intervention with the danger that this might ultimately lead to global war.

The paper conceded that Indochina was 'top priority' for the United States, who nevertheless wanted both to save South East Asia from Communism and to avoid 'deeper American involvement'. Yet there seemed no course of action (and various alternatives were considered) open to the United States that promised success without the risk of further alienating Vietnamese nationalists, swelling the ranks of the Vietminh or proving unacceptable to the French. Bao Dai and others of his kind were broken reeds.

There might thus 'no longer be any prospect of a really

favourable solution . . . the most we can do is to strive for the adoption of the least disadvantageous course'.

The recommendations naturally concentrated on things to avoid: any American involvement deeper than more aid and instructors (which would do neither good nor harm); a cease-fire in present positions; admission of Communists to a coalition government; elections (the wrong side would win) or any form of partition that allowed the Vietminh to reach the Mekong, thus endangering first Siam, then Malaya.

> So long as there is any hope of success we should continue to urge the French to maintain their present policy. . . . If . . . the French are determined to reach a settlement . . . a solution based on the partition of Vietnam and the safeguarding of the independence of Laos and [a late addition this] Cambodia might be best as a *pis aller*'.[22]

If we disregard those sentences inserted only as ritual incantations against the charge of defeatism, *Policy Towards Indochina* has weathered the hindsight of thirty years without too much discredit. It exaggerated – thanks to the Chiefs of Staff, but most people then agreed with them – the dangers of global war;[23] it did not sufficiently emphasise the improbability of success for deeper American involvement, but who could then have foreseen the magnitude of that tragic fiasco? Where it erred most oddly was in predicting a serious divergence of views, before and during the Conference, between the *French* and the Americans, with Britain embarrassed by the need to mediate. Clearly the singular personalities of Bidault and Dulles were not yet fully understood in London.

The rest of the world had not, unfortunately, suspended their own activities in order to await the unfolding of this Whitehall contest. All through the first quarter of 1954 the news from Indochina was depressing: no success for the famous Navarre Plan; too many Vietminh advances; no progress in political negotiations between the French and their Vietnamese allies. The French sought more American help, sent their Minister of Defence and Chairman of the Chiefs of Staff to Indochina on a mission of enquiry, concluded on their return that no degree of reinforcement would ensure success for a military solution[24] and, after the middle of March, began to fear they might face the

prospect of humiliating defeat at Dien Bien Phu. Naturally there
still existed optimists – beside Malcolm Macdonald (whom Eden
now found irritatingly hopeful). On 10 February the United
States Ambassador at Saigon thought it would have a good effect
if Bao Dai sent his son back to Vietnam to train as an officer[25] and
on 21 February General Navarre told the same Ambassador he
hoped the Vietminh would attack Dien Bien Phu.[26]

Gloom naturally spread into the press and, in Britain as in
France, the Berlin Conference was followed by increased
emphasis on the possibility of a negotiated settlement. *The Times*,
despite increasing coverage of Indochina, still took its reports
from Paris and treated the conflict as a French affair, even if some
members of parliament and left-wing publications were becoming
aware of the importance of the American angle.

In fact, American reactions were both sharper and more
significant, though even the British government, let alone press
and members of parliament, did not realise how far the Americans
were carrying their thoughts. On 6 January, for instance,
Robertson, the Assistant Secretary of State for Far Eastern Affairs
and a hard-liner, thought it necessary to warn Dulles, while
advocating further logistic assistance to the French, that 'any
commitment of US forces in Indochina may lead to the eventual
necessity of making progressively larger commitments'.[27] On 8
January, Admiral Radford, Chairman of the US Chiefs of Staff,
was already recommending to the National Security Council
American air intervention at Dien Bien Phu.[28] Public warnings to
China and talk about massive retaliation would have seemed
much more ominous if it had been known that a meeting of the
National Security Council on 16 January had discussed, as a
possible response to hypothetical Chinese intervention in
Indochina, going to war, if necessary alone, with both China and
the Soviet Union.[29] What the Americans did tell the British was
less menacing: their concern that French military efforts were no
longer aimed at victory but at establishing a position for
negotiations; their criticism of French tactics and of French
refusal to accept American help with training; their growing
conviction that they themselves could not stand idly by if
Communism threatened to overpower Indochina. Only on 17
March did Eden circulate to the Cabinet a report from the
Embassy in Washington that Indochina (thus mentioned to the
Cabinet for the first time that year) had become 'top priority' for

the Americans, who were 'baffled and frustrated' because they would neither accept the risk of Communist domination in South East Asia, nor intervene with American combat forces.[30]

The first warning from the Embassy had come a month earlier, when Sir Roger Makins, the Ambassador, said he was constantly being asked about the British attitude to deeper US involvement in Indochina and sought guidance.[31] Denis Allen replied on 24 February, emphasising that his carefully qualified views were personal, but concluding that 'until the Geneva Conference has met, this country would be reluctant to see the United States involve themselves further in Indochina on a scale which seemed to increase the risk of Chinese intervention and thus of extending the war.'[32]

The reference to national opinion was justified. It was not only Eden, who had telegraphed from Berlin his anxiety at the possibly provocative effect of sending US Air Force ground staff to Hanoi to service French military aircraft,[33] who was worried about American intentions. Public concern, much less acute then than it became later, was aroused by American words rather than their deeds. Dulles alone was enough to alarm anyone, so frequent and strident were his public statements, but there was never any shortage of Senators to support or even to surpass him. One of them was Senator Joseph R. McCarthy, whose anti-Communist hysteria was prominently and censoriously reported by *The Times* throughout February and March and did more than many Americans realised to prejudice foreign opinion against their country. But nobody in London seems to have learned that, on 5 March, Senator Symington had suggested the use of atomic bombs to the French Minister of Defence, who doubted whether Indochina offered suitable targets for such weapons.[34]

In France the public emphasis was on negotiation. Laniel, *The Times* reported, had insisted to the National Assembly on 5 March that Indochina must be raised at the outset of the Geneva Conference and his speech – 'nous sommes unanimes en effet, à souhaiter désormais de régler le conflit par voie de négociation' – was well received.[35] On 13 March *The Times* reported a fatal symptom – shelling of the airstrip at Dien Bien Phu – and, for the rest of the month its reports on the battle, in spite of those featuring the parachuting of reinforcements, grew ever more ominous.

What *The Times* did not report and what it seems even the

British government did not know was what the French were up to with the Americans. Two days after the National Assembly had voted for the government motion welcoming the Geneva Conference, the same government decided to send the French Chief of Staff (who was always a soldier in France) to Washington, ostensibly to seek a promise of American support if – it was a familiar French nightmare – the Chinese air force were to intervene in the Indochina conflict.[36] General Ely arrived on 20 March and began by telling Radford that there was an even chance of holding Dien Bien Phu. If it fell, the military consequences would not be serious, but the political repercussions would be grave. On that same day, as it happens, Oliver Harvey, the Ambassador in Paris, maintained that the French would still want a negotiated settlement even if they *held* Dien Bien Phu.[37]

On 22 March Ely also saw Eisenhower. On 24 March, so Ely says, Radford suggested the possibility of sending 60 B29 bombers (then the heaviest American aircraft) to attack the besiegers of Dien Bien Phu[38] subject, so Ely told the French Defence and Foreign Ministers on 27 March, to approval by the US government of a request from the French government for such assistance. On 29 March the French Government decided to send Colonel Brohon to ask General Navarre whether Operation VAUTOUR (a name apparently coined in Saigon) would do the trick.[39] Discussion of the conflict between French and American evidence concerning these contacts may legitimately be postponed to the next chapter, for it continued. What matters now is that the British embassies in Paris and Washington had reported nothing to supplement the story in *The Times* of 27 March that Ely had been discussing the provision of training facilities and the loan of aircraft.

What did come from Washington, on 23 March, was a plea for guidance concerning British policy towards Indochina. In the next few weeks many British missions would make similar requests and most of them would not even get the reply John Tahourdin sent to Washington: it was 'under consideration.'[40] Then, foreshadowed by a warning from Makins on the 27th,[41] came first the Dulles speech of 29 March calling for united action to prevent the imposition of the Communist system on South East Asia and, on 30 March, the message that he would shortly want to discuss the need for the adoption of a clear Anglo-American position to prevent a French sell-out in Indochina.[42]

Obviously agreement had only been reached just in time on British policy towards Indochina: American and French attitudes were crystallising simultaneously. The trouble was that none of the three governments had produced a policy that was intellectually consistent or that they were prepared frankly to disclose to the other two. In principle the French had opted for a negotiated settlement, but were also exploring the possibility of securing American military intervention, something they preferred to conceal, as did the Americans, from the British Government. The United States Government proclaimed their eagerness to do something, but left their Allies uncertain – were probably unsure themselves – what they had in mind: an ultimatum to China, intervention at Dien Bien Phu or something more durable but also more distant in time. They were clear about their need for collective support, less so about the policy to be supported.

As for the British they were still too shamefaced at their new realism frankly to declare a policy that could be attacked as defeatist and incompatible with the principle of Anglo-American solidarity. It did not help when a left-wing MP publicly urged Eden 'to put forward some bold constructive plan which would result in world peace'.[43] The Foreign Office preferred a more subdued approach. The telegram sent to Washington (it was initialled by Lord Reading, the Minister of State) once Eden had approved *Policy Towards Indochina* instructed the Ambassador to draw on that paper when talking to Dulles, but gave him as his uncertain keynote the curious double, if not triple, negative earlier quoted: 'It would be unrealistic not to face the possibility that the conditions for a favourable solution in Indochina may no longer exist'.[44]

That was no way to tell an ambassador notoriously solicitous for the preservation of good Anglo-American relations that the superficially ambivalent paper sent to him was to be interpreted in the manner most displeasing to Mr Dulles. From that telegram stemmed months of misunderstanding and much needless bitterness. As I recorded in my diary at the time: 'my original draft of this was considerably watered down and emerged rather flabby. . . . I think it was a mistake not to tell the Americans exactly what we thought and to do as they always do – begin by stating our maximum position'.

Not for another thirty years did I discover that our timid

telegram had actually crossed one in rather different style from Dulles telling *his* ambassador 'to bring UK to greater recognition of its own responsibilities'.[45] No such knowledge was needed to apply the simple principle enshrined in the international rules for the avoidance of collisions: any change of course should be early and bold enough to be obvious to other vessels.

4 The Crisis of April

'the paralysis of the British Government was almost as serious as that of the French.'—J. F. DULLES, 6 April 1954[1]

John Foster Dulles, since January 1953 Secretary of State under President Eisenhower, was a man whose temperament and formation set him apart from both Bidault and Eden. The experiences those two shared – active military service, national responsibility in the Second World War, getting themselves elected and re-elected – he lacked. Their weaknesses – Bidault's dependence under stress on drink or drugs, the irritable intensity of Eden's vanity – did not afflict Dulles. He was not driven, as they were, by personal ambition. Eden wanted to be Prime Minister and Bidault, who had held that office more than once, believed he could still use it to transform France. Dulles had reached, as he must have known, his personal ceiling and could afford to devote all his efforts to the task he had long desired: the direction of American foreign policy.

In his old-fashioned manner and appearance; his ostentatiously strong principles; his intolerance of opposition; his horror, cool calculations of national interest notwithstanding, of dealings with Communist régimes; in his curious combination of intellectual and moral rigidity with a certain dexterity in everyday conduct; in an odd kind of naïveté; even in the coincidence of making a sister the recipient of political confidences, he resembled another statesman of the same generation (ten years older than either Bidault or Eden) – Neville Chamberlain.

Dulles nevertheless had a more complex personality. Two independent observers who saw him in action in 1954 picked on the same characteristic: 'those who had dealings with him at the time . . . sometimes were at a loss to penetrate his meaning'[2]; 'he can be (and sometimes is) extremely vague in what he says, so that you have little precise idea of what he means to convey, and yet he gives the impression of having a good mind.'[3] Few would have said that of Neville Chamberlain, who usually had the courage not only to express, but to act on, his mistaken convictions. In 1954 Dulles was still seen as a man willing to run great risks in order to uphold his fanatical anti-Communism in all its purity. His actual conduct left contemporary observers uncertain and still puzzles historians. Did he mean what he said, only to be over-ruled by the President or the force of political circumstances? Was it all a calculated bluff, what Denis Allen called 'thunder off for the benefit of congressional critics or the Communist adversary'?[4] Or did the human waywardness this Presbyterian Elder had banished from his private life invade his conduct of public business, leaving him always surer of ends than means?

If he was often misunderstood, one cause was the frequent vehemence of his language, a device doubtless adopted to ensure that his ideas carried more conviction than their sense or clarity might otherwise have sustained. In public statements 'massive retaliation' (which meant a nuclear response to conventional attack) or 'agonising reappraisal' were effective touches of drama, even if the alienation they aroused probably exceeded the enthusiasm. The same applies to the words for which he will be most remembered: 'The ability to get to the verge without getting into war is the necessary art . . . We walked to the brink and we looked it in the face.'[5] Thirty years later 'brinkmanship' is still a pejorative cliché among writers who have forgotten, if they ever knew, that Dulles practised more cautiously than he preached.

This linguistic incontinence was not confined to public platforms. The quotation at the head of this chapter comes from an official report to the National Security Council. Before the April crisis ended President Eisenhower would be told: 'After dinner [Dulles was the host] I hit Eden again'.[6] Shuckburgh understandably called it a 'terrible dinner' and Eden reported, in the blander terms favoured at the Foreign Office, 'we were subjected to a prolonged and, at moments, somewhat heated onslaught on our attitude'.[7] To foreigners all this was rather confusing and Dulles did spread more heat than light.

In the spring of 1954 the Indochina policy of the United States had not changed in essence, but, Indochina being more important to American politicians than to British, the risk that no amount of money would suffice to keep the French fighting till final victory had received high-level consideration in Washington earlier than in London. The thought was even more unpalatable on the other side of the Atlantic, but at least some of the alternatives had been looked at. 'Massive retaliation', Dulles explained on 19 March, did not apply to Indochina.[8] Most responsible leaders also ruled out the commitment of American soldiers on the mainland of Asia: a course which, it was then believed, the experience of the Korean War had shown to be militarily unsound and politically disastrous. Vice-President Nixon, who embarrassed the Administration by telling journalists on 16 April that it might be necessary to take the risk of sending American troops 'to save this embattled land', was an exception.[9]

Rather more American leaders were tempted by the idea put forward by Admiral Radford of using only American air and naval forces, whether against China or the besiegers of Dien Bien Phu. Professional opinion was divided. Vice-Admiral Davis, on the staff of the Secretary of Defense, dismissed the idea of limited intervention as early as January with the comment: 'one cannot go over Niagara Falls in a barrel only slightly'.[10] In April even Radford's colleagues on the Chiefs of Staff Committee were dubious about air intervention at Dien Bien Phu.[11] But discussion did produce agreement that any armed intervention would need Congressional approval, which might not be forthcoming unless the United States had the backing of a respectable coalition of friendly nations. Once Eisenhower had put this idea to the National Security Council on 25 March,[12] the creation of such a coalition came to seem an objective in itself as well as a prior condition for any kind of deeper American involvement. Thus began that confusion of ends and means which was to cause so much misunderstanding in London and Paris. American policy was operating on two tracks.

One track, that of immediate action, had, as explained in the last chapter, been started by Radford's talks with Ely. Radford himself denied he had made any commitment,[13] but the National Security Council tentatively discussed the possibility of an air strike at Dien Bien Phu on 1 April[14] and Dulles is said to have mentioned it to Congressional leaders on 3 April, only to find them opposed to American intervention except as part of a coalition.[15] When Navarre, originally sceptical of its utility, changed his mind and Laniel asked the United States Government for Operation VAUTOUR, he invoked an alleged promise by Radford[16] and the record of a telephone conversation between Eisenhower and Dulles suggests that Radford had said something to give that impression.[17] As Radford himself later commented: 'there was good reason to believe the French were as confused about the real intentions of the United States as we were about those of France'.[18] If a retrospective British account (which put the date of the French request at 2 rather than 4 April) is right in attributing to Dulles the comment that the French request was 'slightly hysterical',[19] this was an unfair description of their response to an American suggestion. But the request was rejected.

The reason given was the need for 'united action', the second track of American policy, which had been publicly inaugurated in the speech made by Dulles to the Overseas Press Club on 29 March. On 2 April Dulles told Makins that the United States Government would not tolerate the loss of South East Asia to Communism. There was still no reason why the Navarre Plan should not succeed, but possible courses of action in case it failed should be considered. When Makins said no good solution might any longer be possible and started to draw on *Policy Towards Indochina*, Bedell Smith, the Under-Secretary of State of whom we shall hear more, dismissed partition as an idea the Americans had already examined and rejected. It does not appear, however, from his report that Makins attempted to argue the case against deeper United States involvement when Dulles went on to say it might be necessary to issue a warning to China, even to threaten naval and air action against the Chinese coast.[20]

Instead Makins telegraphed to Eden that the evolution of United States policy on Indochina had confronted Her Majesty's Government with a major choice. Either we must range ourselves with the fundamental decision taken by the United States, which would enable us to bring our influence continually to bear upon them, or else we must dissociate ourselves from United States policy. In that case they would go ahead without us, gathering such associates as they could. The choice would affect the whole Anglo-United States relationship.[21]

These arguments, which are often addressed to British Foreign Secretaries, impressed Eden. The telegram was followed by a personal message from Eisenhower to Churchill urging the case for united action by Britain, France, the Associated States, Australia and New Zealand, Thailand and the Philippines as well as the United States; arguing that neither Britain nor the United States would need to provide appreciable ground forces and emphasising that Burma, Indonesia and Thailand could not be expected to survive the fall of Indochina, while Malaya, Australia and New Zealand would be directly threatened.[22] Two days later, as doctrinal backing for these assertions, the President unveiled his famous 'domino theory' at a press conference.[23]

This was quite a barrage and it is to Eden's credit that, although his subordinates were divided, he told the United States Ambassador, who came on 6 April to dissuade him from supposing that anything could be achieved at Geneva, that there was no point in being hustled into hasty decisions. Churchill had already sent a stalling reply to Eisenhower, accepting his proposal of a visit by Dulles to explain 'united action'.[24]

In Washington meanwhile Dulles had warned the House of Representatives that continued Chinese help to the Vietminh might call for retaliation, had approached South Korea and Taiwan as well as his declared candidates for 'united action', had received bipartisan support from the Senate and had told the National Security Council that 'the regional grouping . . . was a means of compelling the British to agree to join with us . . . and . . . to reexamine their colonial policy . . . so ruinous to our objectives'.[25]

This last was something the British Cabinet did not know when they assembled on 7 April to discuss the rather different arguments in Eisenhower's letter. Nor were they aware of the rejected French plea for American intervention at Dien Bien Phu (it was that very day that Massigli told Kirkpatrick).[26] But Indochina was now regularly featured on the centre page of *The Times* (news had not yet disturbed the staid dignity of the front page) and, on 6 April, for the first time, Shuckburgh's diary gave that country prominence among Eden's preoccupations. On 8 April Shuckburgh recorded: 'two terrible days . . . the Eisenhower plan for the Far East worrying everybody'.

The Cabinet, told by Eden that the eventual establishment of an organisation for collective defence in South East Asia could be considered but that an immediate warning to China would be dangerous and unnecessary, agreed that Eden should prepare alternative proposals for discussion with Dulles on his arrival.[27] As Shuckburgh recorded in his diary: 'The question is, can we "go along" with him at all on his project?'

That question disturbed and divided those concerned. The arguments put forward by Makins found supporters within the Office, though not in South East Asia Department. *The Times*, which had reported on 6 April a public statement by Dulles that continued Chinese help to the Vietminh might call for retaliation against the Chinese mainland, had a worried first leader 'The Red Light' on 9 April deprecating proposals that assumed the Geneva Conference must fail. The previous day Eden had succeeded in persuading Attlee, the Leader of the Opposition, not to insist on asking a Private Notice Question,[28] but parliamentary pressure was clearly mounting. So it was in Washington, where various Senators called for decisions to be deferred on aid for nations anxious to postpone united action until after Geneva. One such nation was France, whose decision was notified to Eden on 9 April.[29] Australia and New Zealand were equally backward in discharging the task allotted to them by Dulles of putting pressure on the British.[30] Their High Commissioners merely asked for British views and got, in common with governments and British missions all over the world, no satisfactory reply. In that respect at least Dulles was right: until he had been and gone, the Foreign Office would be, in the words I recorded at the time, 'paralysed by indecision'.[31]

The Chiefs of Staff, probably annoyed by having to repeat their earlier advice on a Saturday, were more forthright than ever on 10 April. The campaign in Indochina would not be decided by the fate of Dien Bien Phu. Even if the French held out there, they lacked the resources to establish and maintain control throughout Indochina. The French needed reinforcements, not just the cessation of Chinese aid to their enemies. In any case, threats or action against China would be ineffective short of atomic war and, unless we were prepared for that and the risk of the Russians joining in, we would have to accept either the inclusion of Communists in a coalition government or else the partition of Indochina. Partition was the lesser evil.[32]

Then, on Sunday 11 April, Dulles and his team arrived in London for a singularly unfortunate series of discussions. Three weeks earlier, so Dulles explained, the United States Chiefs of Staff had recommended air and naval intervention in Indochina and carriers had been deployed from Manila, but Dulles had taken the view that two prior measures were needed to make intervention politically acceptable: full independence for the Associated States (Bao Dai arrived in Paris for the Vietnamese negotiations that very Sunday) and the declaration by an appropriate group of countries of their readiness for united action.

If these conditions were met, he was confident Congress would authorise the President to use air and naval forces, possibly even land forces, in Indochina.[33] Dulles did not specify the nature of the military operations envisaged, but concentrated on obtaining Eden's consent to an immediate declaration of common purpose. The idea of an explicit warning to China had receded into the background.

Eden said Her Majesty's Government could make no commitments before the Geneva Conference and expressed his doubt that any allied intervention could be confined to the air and sea.[34] Unfortunately neither Dulles nor Eden proceeded to explore this fundamental difference in approach. Eden raised the idea of widening Asian participation in any eventual united action by mentioning Burma, India and Pakistan. Dulles jumped into what bridge-players call a shut-out bid with Taiwan, Korea and Japan (politically as suspect in Britain as Eden's candidates in the United States) but the subject was not pursued.[35] Instead, as so often happens when decision-makers confront one another directly, they concentrated on drafting an agreed communiqué. The meat of this, sandwiched between deploring the activities of Communist forces in Indochina and hoping the Geneva Conference would lead to the restoration of peace, was: 'we are ready to take part, with the other countries principally concerned, in an examination of the possibility of establishing a collective defence. . .'.

Both principals regarded this vacuous formula as an achievement. Eden told the ad hoc group of Ministers who approved the draft on the evening of 12 April that he had kept out any commitment to direct military intervention in Indochina.[36] Dulles reported he had moved 'the British away from their original position that nothing should be said or done before Geneva'.[37] Most of those concerned in London agreed with Dulles. There was dismay in South East Asia Department and, in the House of Commons, Aneurin Bevan, then the leader of the Left, declared that Eden's statement on his conversations with Dulles, which had been received with hostile interjections from the Opposition, 'will be deeply resented by the majority of people in Great Britain . . . a surrender to American pressure'.[38] Two days later *The Times* reported he had resigned from the Shadow Cabinet because Attlee, the leader of the Labour Party, had failed to 'repudiate Mr Eden's acceptance of the American initiative'.

There had been 13 Parliamentary Questions on the Dulles visit, all pro-Geneva, and it was left to *The Times* to argue that a stampede into security precautions had been avoided.

Dulles, for his part, went off to Paris (he had rejected Eden's earlier proposal for a tripartite meeting) and told Bidault on 14 April 'the United Kingdom had indicated they would take part at once in an informal working group in Washington in which their Ambassador would participate'. Bidault replied that nothing could be done before Geneva,[39] but the next day Eden had to deny a story the French Ambassador in London had heard from his United States colleague: at dinner with Churchill private assurances had been given to Dulles of British willingness to make a military contribution to joint intervention in Indochina.[40] American achievements were undergoing improvement.

Even before this Eden, evidently uneasy about the way the talks had gone, had asked for a draft telegram instructing Makins to impress Eden's views on the United States Government before their own ideas hardened. It went off without the more explicit paragraphs drafted by South East Asia Department, but with a characteristic double negative: 'I am not convinced that no concession could be made to Communists in Indochina without inevitably leading to Communist domination of the whole of South East Asia, particularly if we have the proposed security system'. Such language was not welcome in Washington and, when challenged, Makins surprisingly told the State Department he did not think it applied to proceedings at Geneva.[41]

Then came the explosion. The same telegram reported that Dulles would call a meeting of the Ambassadors of Australia, Britain, France, New Zealand, the Philippines, Thailand and the Associated States on 20 April, when he would describe the results of his talks in London and Paris and propose the establishment of an informal working group. 'I presume' Makins ended 'that I can agree to such a proposal'.

Unfortunately for the Ambassador, 16 April 1954, when he sent that telegram, was Good Friday. When it reached the Foreign Office on Easter Saturday, there was no official available capable of controlling Eden. That day and the next he sent Makins six telegrams he had drafted himself.[42] Only the last of these, with its well-known sentence 'Americans may think the time past when they need consider the feelings or difficulties of their allies', was quoted in Eden's own account.[43] He was prudent not to reproduce the preceding words: 'I am not aware that Dulles has any cause for complaint'. Eden told the Ambassador not to attend; accused Dulles, whose interpretation of the London talks was, as Makins inviting Burma; complained of not being consulted; asked why the meeting could not be in London instead and reluctantly accepted that the meeting was already public knowledge and could not be cancelled, merely turned into one of the 16 nations concerned with Korea. It was still 'dangerous and ill-timed'. Some of Eden's remarks, including the admonition to Dulles to stick to the communiqué when talking about his trip and the parting shot already quoted, Makins probably kept to himself.[44]

Although Dulles received the news calmly, he resented and continued to resent Eden's action in forbidding Makins to attend the meeting and Eden's insistence that Dulles had jumped the gun in arranging it. He told his sister 'Eden has reversed himself and gone back on his agreement'.[45] Eden never admitted it, but Dulles, whose interpretation of the London talks was, as Makins commented at the time, supported by the 'clear and unequivocal' American record as opposed to the ambiguous British version, was probably right.[46] On 13 April, for instance, Dulles had reported Eden as saying that an informal working group in Washington was a good idea and Makins would be available.[47] What happened was that Eden, already uneasy at the extent to which Dulles had manoeuvred him towards the slippery slope, simply lost his temper when he read the telegram from Makins (whose tendency to see the American point of view irritated Eden). The replies he fired off were the petulant reaction of a cornered rabbit. It was a deplorable performance and it lastingly impaired relations between Eden and Dulles, but it did check the dangerous drift towards a futile war. Although the United States would subsequently return to the charge again and again, Eden's Easter outburst may reasonably be regarded as the turning-point of the April crisis. Henceforth Eden had a personal position to defend.

At the time and in his memoirs the main justification advanced by Eden for his conduct was that the meeting envisaged by Dulles would have confined membership of the proposed security organisation to those then invited and made it impossible to recruit other Asian, particularly Commonwealth, participants. This is a slightly suspect argument. It is true that, on 8 April, Eden had been disappointed by the advice he received from Denis

Allen: it would be no good asking any Asian country except the Philippines and Thailand (the two chosen by Dulles) to join in 'collective action'.[48] But Eden's attitude to wider Asian participation had not previously been enthusiastic. A telegram from Djakarta reporting Indonesian interest in being represented at Geneva elicited a minute on 17 March from Eden: 'we don't want any of these folk. We have enough already and more'.[49] When the High Commissioner in Delhi urged that Nehru should be kept informed of British views, Eden minuted on 10 April: 'But why?'[50] On 15 April Eden described Nehru (regarded by the Americans as the evil spirit influencing Eden) as a 'miserable little Indian Kerensky'.[51]

To some extent Eden must subsequently have been converted to the view that the participation of Burma, Ceylon, India, Indonesia and Pakistan in the right kind of collective security organisation in South East Asia was both desirable and possible. Nothing else would explain the time and trouble, including a constant flow of personal messages, devoted to keeping these governments informed of proceedings at Geneva and plans for South East Asian defence. To begin with, however, the idea may have appealed to him mainly as a justification for saying no, and going on saying no, to repeated American proposals for British participation in military adventures before and, indeed, instead of the Geneva Conference. As an argument with some positive appeal it was the counterpart of American insistence that they could not do anything except as part of a 'united action'.

The Americans, however, always regarded Eden's emphasis on the need for wider Asian participation as the merest pretext for obstruction and delay: partly because they were angry with Eden, partly because they rightly considered it improbable that any of the countries favoured by Eden would ever participate in any arrangement acceptable to the United States. In the end the only one to join the South East Asia Treaty Organisation was Pakistan: a source of embarrassment as long as that rather useless alliance lasted.

Preferring the desirable to the merely feasible could have been defended, but Eden did not help himself by telling Dulles, the next time they met on 22 April (Eden's own account does not admit to the first ten words): '*when he had agreed in London to informal working group*, he had overlooked Colombo Conference [of the five favoured Asian Prime Ministers] which opens April 26'.[52]

The Easter outburst was naturally reflected in *The Times*, where Our Diplomatic Correspondent speculated that the British Government might not favour talks in Washington about defence in South East Asia until India, Pakistan and Ceylon had been consulted. The first leader, 'Outlook Uncertain', on 19 April linked McCarthy, Nixon and Dulles in a somewhat apprehensive survey of United States foreign policy.

There was greater cause for anxiety in Paris, where Eden, arriving on 22 April for a NATO meeting, found himself involved in three days of hurried conversations, sometimes with both Bidault and Dulles, sometimes with only one of them, about alarming news from Indochina and startling French and American proposals. The confusion caused by the fragmentary nature of the discussion is reflected in the conflicting American, British and French accounts of what went on. What made it worse was that Bidault was sometimes drunk: 'in a state of great exhaustion'[53] on 22 April; 'very tired' on the 23rd.[54] His weakness was notorious and President Auriol has recorded a spectacular instance in which Bidault was not only unable to continue his speech in the Chamber, but collapsed onto one of the Communist benches.[55]

Dulles started the ball rolling by telling Eden on arrival that the French Government were all but determined to quit the fight in Indochina altogether. His own enquiries convinced Eden this was exaggerated and he concluded that Dulles had upset Bidault by again tackling him about 'united action' at a time when Bidault could think only of Dien Bien Phu.[56] This seems plausible, for subsequent discussions proceeded on these two tracks. The next day Dulles was shown a telegram from Navarre requesting an immediate and massive American air intervention as the only way of saving Dien Bien Phu and the only alternative to Navarre's seeking a cease-fire in Indochina. Dulles considered this out of the question, but referred it to President Eisenhower with the characteristic comment 'France is almost visibly collapsing under our eyes'.[57] At 9 p.m. on 24 April his written refusal was delivered to Bidault: it would be unconstitutional without Congressional approval; it would not suffice to save Dien Bien Phu; the fall of Dien Bien Phu would not materially and vitally alter the military position in Indochina.

Admiral Radford, also in Paris, took a different line. In his view the whole military situation in Indochina would get out of control within days of the fall of Dien Bien Phu.[58] Although, when asked by General Ely for Operation VAUTOUR, he pretended (Dulles did not) not to know what that was,[59] he told Eden that Britain and the United States should take over the Indochina war; asked about the availability of RAF squadrons and a British carrier and suggested Navarre would have to be removed and the Americans given a voice in operational planning and in training.[60] There is no British or American confirmation of the French story, vouched for by Bidault and two others, that Dulles offered Bidault two atomic bombs for use at Dien Bien Phu. Ely thought it did not make military sense,[61] but Radford himself had tentatively suggested the use of atomic bombs to the National Security Council on 7 April.[62]

What Dulles did do was to start down the second track before he was even ready to reject Bidault's request for intervention at Dien Bien Phu. On 24 April he showed Eden and Bidault the draft of a letter he proposed to address to Bidault: the United States Government would be prepared, if the French Government and their other Allies so desired, to obtain special powers from Congress to move armed forces into Indochina and thus to internationalise the struggle in Indochina and protect South East Asia as a whole.

United action was back with a bang. After some hesitation Bidault, who was still primarily interested in Dien Bien Phu, agreed that Dulles should send him such a letter.[63]

Eden, for his part, decided to return to London to consult his colleagues on the major choice that would now confront them. He did so without any hesitation at all, for Churchill had proposed that he himself should come to Paris. Although Eden's memoirs celebrate the unanimity existing on this occasion as on others between Churchill and himself, he had been one of the Ministers who had decided on 5 April 'that Churchill can in no circumstances be allowed to attend a Top Level Conference'.[64] That was after, as Dulles put it, 'Churchill had almost collapsed in Parliament'.[65]

Having reached agreement with Churchill on the Saturday night, Eden expounded the situation as he saw it on the morning of Sunday 25 April to a meeting of those Ministers who were available together with the Chiefs of Staff.

He told them the military situation in Indochina was extremely grave. The French garrison at Dien Bien Phu would shortly be overwhelmed or compelled to surrender. Dulles feared the collapse of all French resistance in Indochina. To avert this he wanted a dramatic gesture of Anglo-American intervention in Indochina. Dulles had proposed a joint assurance of support to the French and some immediate military assistance. Eden did not believe the kind of intervention proposed would be either militarily or politically effective, a view with which the Chiefs of Staff agreed.

Eden accordingly proposed that Ministers should approve an eight point directive (which Denis Allen had drafted for him in Paris):

(1) We do not regard the London communiqué[66] as committing us to join in immediate discussions on the possibility of Allied intervention in the Indochina war.

(2) We are not prepared to give any undertaking now, in advance of the Geneva Conference, concerning United Kingdom military action in Indochina.

(3) But we shall give all possible diplomatic support to the French delegation at Geneva in efforts to reach an honourable settlement.

(4) We can give an assurance now that if a settlement is reached at Geneva, we shall join in guaranteeing that settlement and in setting up a collective defence in South East Asia, as foreshadowed in the London communiqué, to make that joint guarantee effective.

(5) We hope that any Geneva settlement will make it possible for the joint guarantee to apply to at least the greater part of Indochina.

(6) If no such settlement is reached, we shall be prepared at that time to consider with our allies the action to be taken jointly in the situation then existing.

(7) But we can not give any assurance now about possible action on the part of the United Kingdom in the event of failure to reach agreement at Geneva for the cessation of hostilities in Indochina.

(8) We shall be ready to join with the United States Government now in studying measures to ensure the defence of Thailand and the rest of South East Asia, including Malaya, in the event of all or part of Indochina being lost.

The adoption of this admirable statement (so clear, concise and comprehensive) of British policy effectively determined the outcome of the April crisis, though it still had to be defended against allies who, having foolishly manoeuvred themselves into a position where they had to accept a British veto, could nevertheless protest – and did so. It goes without saying that much trouble would have been avoided if anything comparably explicit had been communicated to Dulles, or even to Bidault, at at earlier stage. Unfortunately some truths become self-evident to politicians – to human beings, for that matter – only when their back has been firmly pressed against the wall.

The first counter-attack came that afternoon, when Eden told those Ministers and Chiefs of Staff still available of a communication he had just received from Massigli, the French Ambassador in London. Bedell Smith had told the French Ambassador in Washington that, if Britain would join in a declaration of common purpose, Eisenhower would seek Congressional authority and try to attack the besiegers of Dien Bien Phu on 28 April. The French Government hoped Britain would agree.

Churchill said what we were being asked to do was in effect to aid in misleading Congress into approving a military operation which would itself be ineffective and might well bring the world to the verge of major war. This request must be rejected.[67] Given the terms in which Dulles had refused, less than 24 hours earlier, the French request for intervention at Dien Bien Phu, Churchill's verdict was justified.

When Eden was finally able to leave, that evening, for Geneva, he had earned his special RAF aircraft. Admittedly he could have been bolder earlier and have avoided the scandal of the Easter outburst. But it should be remembered that most of those with access to Eden and influence over him tended to favour conformity with American policies. Reading and South East Asia Department, who took a more independent line, carried little weight. Denis Allen, who carried much, was initially hesitant. It did not help that public opposition to American plans came mainly from the Left. Eden's motives may not always have been pure or his conduct blameless, but he did more than anyone else to ensure that April, for Britain, ended in peace.

French reactions were milder than might have been expected. Bidault was not surprised, when he was told of the eight points that evening, and his complaint on 30 April that France was left on her own was common form. From Paris, on the same day, the Embassy reported a sense of relief that the British had refused to let the Americans internationalise the war. Raymond Aron, then as later the most eminent French writer on international relations, remarked on 3 May, the day the April crisis ended with the return of Dulles to Washington, that American policy was a mixture of 'rhetoric, intransigence and inaction'. He was less certain whether the British had shown their wisdom or only their cynicism.[68]

Dulles, on the other hand, found the eight point statement 'most disheartening', when told of it by Eden late on 25 April.[69] The next day he again pressed Eden for military discussions;[70] on 27 April he accused Eden of pushing the French towards a cease-fire[71] and on the 28th he lost his temper, when Eden showed him the text of Churchill's parliamentary statement that there would be no military commitments before the outcome of the Geneva Conference was known, and stalked out of the house without a word.[72] As he reported to Washington on 29 April: 'UK attitude is one of increasing weakness. Britain seem to feel that we are disposed to accept present risks of a Chinese war and this, coupled also with their fear that we would start using atomic weapons, has badly frightened them'.[73]

By 30 April, after another tirade from Dulles, even Evelyn Shuckburgh, whose concern for good Anglo-American relations always made him anxious to see Eden taking a more conciliatory line, described 'the almost pathological rage and gloom of Foster Dulles'. His vehemence was probably self-defeating, for Eden, though easily over-impressed by dominant personalities, reacted badly to being denounced. In spite of three telegrams from Makins warning that Dulles might seek Congressional authority to proceed with his plans without British cooperation,[74] Eden put an end to the April crisis on 3 May when he told the Cabinet, who agreed, 'we must decline to be drawn into the war in Indochina or even into promising moral support for measures of intervention of which the full scope is not yet known'.[75] After again attempting to mobilise Australia and New Zealand under the ANZUS banner Dulles left Geneva at the end of what the *Washington Evening Star* called one of 'the most disastrous weeks in the history of American diplomacy'.[76]

5 Geneva: Tuning Up

'we drove to the hotel which the British Foreign Secretary has always used.'—ANTHONY EDEN[1]

Geneva is accustomed to international conferences and on this occasion Swiss hospitality was supplemented by the United Nations Organisation. Although officially concerned only with Korea, they were equally ready to assist discussions on Indochina with the services of the secretariat, the interpreters and the buildings they maintained in Geneva. These last, which had been inherited from the League of Nations, rather resembled, in their heavy pomp, those constructed in Berlin by Albert Speer for the Third Reich, though they had undergone considerable internal modernisation. Space was more ample and less cluttered, but the designers seemed to have been inspired by the public rooms of a transatlantic liner.

Eden was thoroughly at home in Geneva, but this was nevertheless an unusual conference. Chinese Communists, for instance, had not previously been seen in the West. Now some 200 had arrived and, to the surprise of the Swiss, had refused to share a hotel with the Russians. Their leader, Chou en Lai, then Prime Minister as well as Foreign Minister, took the large and splendid villa of Le Grand Mont-Fleuri at Versoix, some seven kilometres from Geneva. Bidault, Eden (belatedly realising that the Hôtel Beau Rivage offered inadequate security against the eavesdroppers of the post-war era) and Molotov found similar abodes. Chauvel, the French Ambassador in Berne and the second man in the French delegation, thought Eden, whom he used to find in slippers in the garden, had the best of them: Le Reposoir.[3]

The Americans huddled together in the Hôtel du Rhône, but the offices and subordinate staffs of the remaining Great Powers were accommodated separately. This helped to spark a memorable fit of temper by Eden, the morning after his arrival,

66

when he discovered that the Delegation offices in the Villa Les Ormeaux had a better view (across the lake and, on the few clear days, as far as Mont Blanc) than his own hotel. It was a relief to all concerned when the Edens (Churchill had agreed that Mrs Eden should accompany him at public expense, an unusual concession in those days, because of the precarious state of his health) moved into Le Reposoir, together with his private secretaries, Harold Caccia and Denis Allen, on 29 April.[4] Harold Caccia, an athletic Old Etonian and a man of dominating personality, was then a Deputy Under-Secretary, but owed much of his influence over Eden to the fact that he had once been his Assistant Private Secretary. Lord Reading was left in the hotel, which also accommodated other members of what, by the modest standards of those days, was quite a large British delegation: it had to cope with Korea as well as Indochina.

Even the Russians, so soon after Stalin's death, were a rarity in Geneva and they attracted almost as much attention as the Chinese. Casey, the Australian Minister of External Affairs, in Geneva for the Korean conference but equally interested in Indochina, recorded in his diary on 27 April: 'The entry and exit of the Russian, Chinese and North Korean delegations to and from the Palais des Nations building in Geneva has to be seen to be believed. They form up in a solid phalanx with strong-arm men in front, behind and on the flanks – fellows like gorillas with their right hands menacingly in their coat pockets.[5] He could have added that the bullet-proof cars used by Chou en Lai and Molotov were initially followed not only by back-up cars containing their own men, but by a Swiss military escort. Dulles was almost as well protected.

It was Eden, going about with a single detective seated beside his female driver, who made all three look faintly ridiculous and provoked a marked, if gradual reduction in the strength and visibility of their escorts.

What disappointed the Swiss and those junior diplomats with too little to do was the absence of any entertaining on the scale made famous by the Congress of Vienna. Social contacts with Communists were abhorrent to the Americans as they were, under the impact of Dien Bien Phu, to the French. The British were alone in being in diplomatic relations with everyone except the Vietminh, but even they confined themselves to small working luncheons and dinners. If rumour had any basis in fact, the worst sufferers were the Russian typists, who complained of having to eat caviare every day, so vast were the stocks – of this and other delicacies – imported by their delegation in the expectation of constant banquets.

There was time enough for such observations, for the Indochina Conference did not begin until 8 May. This had nothing to do with the Colombo Conference of Asian Prime Ministers, which merely generated a brisk exchange of telegrams. What delayed the discussion of Indochina was primarily the question of participation. The French had difficulty in rounding up delegates from the Associated States, whose governments, particularly the Vietnamese, were suspicious of the Conference and apprehensive about its likely outcome. Eden was not very sympathetic towards their efforts to negotiate conditions for their attendance and when Nguyen Quoc Dinh arrived in Geneva on 1 May to represent the Saigon government, only the most junior member of the British delegation was sent to the station to meet him. Finding myself among serried ranks of senior Americans and Frenchmen I appointed myself the personal representative of the Secretary of State and delivered an invented message of greeting from Eden.

These Vietnamese were, of course, also the principal objectors to Vietminh participation in the Conference. Bidault constantly altered his own attitude and on 27 April Dulles, of all people, had to join with Eden to tell him it was inevitable. As Dulles remarked to Eden, the French were in a hopeless mood and needed guidance.[6] On 5 May Eden, still trying to get the Conference started, complained that the French were suffering from growing inability to make up their minds on any subject.[7] That was, for instance, their initial reaction to Molotov's proposal that the chairmanship of the Conference should alternate between Eden and himself.[8] After his bruising experiences with Dulles Eden found Molotov surprisingly reasonable, even helpful, as well as being more decisive than Bidault.

Naturally Bidault had problems of his own, with Dien Bien Phu at its last gasp and the Laniel Government, accused of insufficient enthusiasm for a negotiated settlement, experiencing some difficulty in getting a vote of confidence in the National Assembly. 'Le gouvernement ne subsistait que parce qu'il ne réussissait pas à tomber'.[9] From Paris both the British and United States embassies independently predicted that French public opinion would force any French government to withdraw from Indochina on any terms that could be negotiated.[10] Nor were Bidault and the representatives of the Associated States alone in setting conditions for the opening of the Conference. Dulles had been adamant that no American should sit at the same table as the Red Chinese. If this was fanaticism, it was also, given the political mood in the United States, self-protection. The problem was overcome by the provision of a separate little table for each delegation, as shown in the photograph of the opening session.

Dulles could not press his objections too far. Although much better off than Bidault, he was, Makins reported on 28 April, in a difficult political situation at home. Having got Congressional leaders, press and public opinion steamed up to support 'united action', this had never materialised. When nothing happened, disillusionment set in and Americans were now confused and uncertain.[11] On 2 May it was the turn of the *Washington Post* to write of 'a major defeat for American diplomacy' and to blame too many political appointments in the State Department and the influence of Senator McCarthy. Dulles himself blamed it on Radford[12] (as did *The Times* on the same day – 5 May).

When the Indochina Conference finally began on 8 May, immediately after the news, so shattering to the French delegation, of the fall of Dien Bien Phu, Eden enjoyed a firmer domestic base than either his American or his French colleague. It was not only the Cabinet, *The Times* (much more interested in Indochina than in Korea) and, with little open dissent, the Conservative Party, who were behind him. He had considerable backing in the Labour Party and, what was more important to so avid and sensitive a newspaper reader as Eden, in the British press as a whole. On 8 May even the acidulous *New Statesman*, which normally denounced, as a reflex action, the policies of any British Government, Conservative or Labour, wrote that it all depended on Eden.

Without Eden it is unlikely that the first session on Indochina would have begun at Geneva on 8 May. Nobody else in the British delegation had the authority and no other non-Communist delegation was consistently and wholeheartedly in favour of the Conference. His success was nevertheless not a foregone conclusion. One of its conditions was the arrival on 1 May, while the orchestra was still tuning up at Geneva, of Bedell Smith to replace Dulles as leader of the United States delegation.

General Walter Bedell Smith had been Chief of Staff during the Second World War to General Eisenhower and President Eisenhower appointed him Undersecretary of State in January 1953 – Number Two to Dulles. It is intriguing to speculate what might have happened if Eisenhower had given him the top job. Certainly this book would have been different. As the principal staff officer of a multinational expeditionary force Bedell Smith had been much admired and retained many friends on both sides of the Atlantic. After he arrived in Geneva Eden had to resist an embarrassing proposal from Churchill to invite Bedell Smith to spend the weekend at Chequers. It was, of course, Churchill and not Bedell Smith whose influence Eden feared in such an encounter. Eden, as he emphasises in his memoirs, liked and admired Bedell Smith.

From the moment of his arrival at Geneva Bedell Smith reinforced the favourable impression already entertained by Eden, whom he told on 1 May 'not to pay too much attention to some of the stupid things being said in the USA'.[13] At the 'terrible dinner with Dulles' that evening, only Bedell Smith showed any comprehension.[14] On 3 May he was 'sympathetic';[15] on 4 May 'reasonable and receptive';[16] on 5 May Eden made a concession to Bedell Smith – the proposal for discussion by the Five Power Staff Agency – he had not, and might not have made to Dulles.[17] Even *The Times* expected only good from the replacement of Dulles by Bedell Smith. On 6 May Makins felt obliged to warn Eden that Bedell Smith might be easier to handle than Dulles, but Dulles had more influence with the President.[18] Six years later Eden called Bedell Smith 'a splendid friend throughout'.[19]

In the course of this narrative we shall see, as Eden could not, what Bedell Smith was actually reporting to his own government about British policy, the British people and Eden himself. Some of his remarks will inevitably provoke the question: was the American a hypocrite and the Englishman a dupe? This seems, on the evidence available, an exaggerated deduction. Bedell Smith had qualities Dulles lacked. He was broad-minded and he had the good manners, the good sense and the natural diplomacy often found in the better type of soldier. But he was an American with his full share of patriotic prejudice. He was not required to love and believe Eden: only to understand him and be polite to him.

Chauvel, the French professional diplomat, provided a good portrait of Bedell Smith:

un homme assez petit, maigre, avec une figure en bosses et ravines qui lui donnait l'apparence d'avoir mâché une pastille amère. En fait . . . il souffrait de l'estomac, ce qui lui valait des crises et des accés d'humeur violents et brefs . . . un homme intelligent, appréciant le concret, comprenant la politique et ne se payant pas de fausse monnaie.[20]

No great degree of hyperacidity was needed for occasional impatience, even indignation, with Eden, but it was a great advantage that Bedell Smith was less inclined than Dulles to deceive himself.

6   Prelude and Fugue

'The most dangerous crisis since the end of the world war.'—
THE TIMES, 17 May 1954

At Geneva, where no two delegations shared the same angle of
vision, each experienced a different Conference. For all of them,
however, there were three distinct preoccupations: the formal
proceedings; the wheeling and dealing behind the scenes; the
protection of one's back. If these assumed particular intensity for
Eden, it was because he was more widely involved. He entered the
arena not just as the leader of a delegation, but as the
representative of a Great Power and as one of the two chairmen.
When he talked to Molotov or Chou en Lai, he had to bear in mind
the views of those delegates who could not, or who would not,
follow his example; his conversations with Bidault or Bedell Smith
were constrained by the sense of a commitment to negotiated
settlement they did not entirely share. And, if other delegates
might sometimes envy his popularity, his back was exposed to
more various arrows: from his allies, from the Old
Commonwealth and from the New, from his rivals in the
Conservative Party and his opponents in the Labour Party, from
all the newspapers to which he was so sensitive, even from the
subdued, the deferential, the barely implied criticism of his own
subordinates.

The plenary sessions which began the Conference offered the
various delegations the opportunity to adopt an attitude. These
were formal occasions: numerous advisers sitting behind the
delegates; prepared speeches; simultaneous translation; verbatim
records compiled, typed, duplicated and distributed in quantity
by the United Nations secretariat. Long before this mass of paper,
which few of its recipients ever read in full, was available, indeed
as soon as each session ended, the spokesmen of the different
delegations were expounding their own versions to the
representatives of the media. These accounts were shorter, more

dramatic, very selective and often strikingly different. The spokesmen had an appreciative audience, for the much publicised Anglo-American-French disputes of the last few weeks had made the Conference news. From Paris and Washington, even from Moscow and Peking, the Embassies telegraphed regular summaries of what actually appeared in the press. And Eden, of course, read all the British newspapers.

In plenary session, therefore, delegates took care to utter no word which might not be read by their political supporters or their political opponents at home. They were not arguing with other delegates, let alone trying to persuade them or hinting at a bargain. At best they were debating.

This speech-making might be tedious, but it was not entirely pointless. At Geneva the participants were not traversing well-trodden ground. Indochina was a new subject for international discussion and the positions of the various governments concerned were neither clearly defined nor well understood. When Bidault, at the opening session on 8 May, called for the regrouping of opposing forces in Vietnam, a cease-fire, the release of prisoners, the disarmament of irregulars and international supervision, he gave French objectives a definition they had hitherto lacked. Pham van Dong, the Vietminh leader, had a point when, at the next session on 10 May, he complained of the absence of French political proposals and commented that Bidault had taken no account of the actual military situation in formulating such measures as he had suggested. By the time Pham van Dong had finished demanding the independence of Cambodia, Laos and Vietnam; elections to create an unified government in each country and the withdrawal of foreign forces; the whole to be preceded by a cease-fire supervised by bilateral commissions only; the nature and extent of the gap separating the French from their adversaries was clearer than before.[1]

Unfortunately it was also wider and, because all the Communist delegates were unsparing in their condemnation of the historical record of Western dealings with South East Asia, now seemed even harder to bridge. The Americans were particularly sensitive to any criticism that ranked them with European colonialists and Dulles had bitterly reproached Eden for his failure to defend the United States against such attacks in the first week of the Korean debate.[2] On 10 May, therefore, Eden thought it prudent expressly to dissent from Pham van Dong's description of the Americans as imperialists and interventionists. His speech of 12 May, when he exhorted delegates to forget history and concentrate on practical problems, particularly regrouping, special treatment for Cambodia and Laos, disarmament of irregulars and international supervision (perhaps enlisting the Colombo Powers) was more characteristic of his deliberately low-key and unpolemical approach.[3]

Eden was not a natural orator. For the preparation of a speech in the House of Commons he needed the assistance of half a dozen officials for hours on end. At Geneva something so simple as 'I propose that we should now adjourn our meeting and reassemble at 3 p.m. on . . .' had to be typed, in triple spacing on blue crested paper using the special machine with extra large characters, for him to read out. This lack of the politician's normal fluency made Eden's speeches distinctly dull, but preserved him from the public temptations of the glib.

He was more at ease in confidential negotiation, quick to respond to his interlocutor, practised in encouraging an atmosphere of relaxed intimacy. Shuckburgh, indeed, thought Eden allowed himself, at dinner, to be over-impressed by Molotov's relative amiability and himself to become too friendly and conciliatory.[4] It is unlikely, however, that Eden was under any lasting illusion. He had seen a good deal of Molotov before Geneva and the Russian was already a legend.

Molotov was not merely a veteran politician, his first term in Siberia coinciding with Eden's first term at Eton, he had undergone a hardening and toughening process without a Western parallel for its length and rigour. Simply to have survived, as a member of Stalin's Politburo, for 28 years was an achievement in itself. He had been Prime Minister and, for two separate spells, Foreign Minister, in which capacity he had negotiated the Nazi-Soviet Pact, organised aggression against Finland, Poland and the Baltic States, attended all the principal post-war conferences and become famous as the Russian who never gave an inch and always said *nyet*: 'stonebottom' Molotov. Since 1953 he had been widely regarded in the West as co-equal with Malenkov, sharing the inheritance of Stalin. His remarkable toughness would later enable him to survive his fall from power, his exile, his expulsion from the Communist Party – to which he was readmitted in 1984 at the age of 94.

This formidable man – his name, chosen by himself, meant

'hammer' – hardly looked the part. A respectable professor in pince-nez, he sat there chain-smoking, stolid and imperturbable. As Chauvel remarked, he spoke in a flat voice, never showed pleasure or displeasure, at most an occasional sense of irony. He was once seen to laugh – during the final night of the Conference.[5]

He and Eden soon found themselves in a special relationship (which had to be personal, for Molotov would not receive a subordinate and it was no use talking to anyone else in the Soviet delegation): not only as the two Co-Chairmen concerned with the procedural aspects of the Conference, but as caucus managers trying to find a basis for compromise on matters of substance. Superficially Molotov had a less unruly team than Eden, but even at the time it was apparent that he could not simply give orders to Chou en Lai and Pham van Dong. The extent of their real independence has since become much clearer as a result of the revelations produced by the Sino-Soviet split (scarcely suspected in 1954) and the conflict between China and Vietnam. Eden, for his part, had to exert his utmost powers of persuasion to influence Bidault and Bedell Smith and relied on Bidault to manage the Associated States, with whose delegates he had few personal dealings.

On all fundamental issues, of course, Eden and Molotov were opposed. What they shared was a reluctance to risk war over issues of secondary importance to British and Russian national interests. Each thought – as Molotov's actions rather than words ultimately revealed – that his allies might reasonably be expected to make some concessions to promote a negotiated settlement. It was clearly Molotov, for instance, who decided not 'officiously to keep alive' the demand Pham van Dong had made on the opening day of the Conference for the representation of resistance movements in Cambodia and Laos: the Khmer Issarak and Pathet Lao.

Earlier, on 7 May, Eden had first to persuade Bidault (who had not been answering for two days) to agree to start discussing Indochina on the 8th, clear this with Bedell Smith, then obtain Molotov's concurrence. Molotov probably enjoyed seasoning his consent with the words: 'I think you are the man who has all the difficulties at this conference'.[6] He was helpful and reasonable about official languages and such matters.[7] So he was on 14 May, before the Fourth Plenary Session, in facilitating agreement that the Conference should try to make faster progress by going into

Restricted Session on 17 May. This he announced, as Chairman, at the end of a Plenary Session in which he had delivered, as Soviet delegate, a speech described by Bidault as 'a diatribe'.[8] Whereas Eden tried to maintain an uniformly reasonable tone, Molotov confined this to private conversation. His formal speeches were unbending and the Soviet press had never heard of any other point of view.

The British press was something Eden did not have to worry about during the first half of May. Newspapers, no less than letters arriving in Geneva from members of the public, supported his policies. Even the Conservative Party had not started to rumble. American and French opinions were less flattering, but the position of their governments was also less assured. It was not a sign of strength that Eisenhower had to pronounce Dulles 'the greatest Secretary of State within his memory'[9] – which must have included Acheson and Marshall. Nor was the survival, on 13 May, of the Laniel Government by two votes anything to be proud of.[10] Eden disregarded the advice of Malcolm Macdonald, on 7 May, to treat seriously the views of that 'shrewd and far-seeing statesman', Bao Dai. Not only had Eden become distinctly disenchanted with the ever-bubbling optimism of Malcolm Macdonald (commended to Churchill by Admiral Radford as the foremost expert on South East Asia),[11] but he despised Bao Dai and thought Ho Chi Minh would win any free election in Vietnam.[12]

This left a lot of people to be kept sweet. There were the Asian Commonwealth countries, who received a constant flow of messages, and the Old Commonwealth countries, whose representatives in Geneva attended the morning meetings at which Denis Allen informed the British delegation of what had been going on behind the scenes. And there were the casuals: all the visitors, particularly the visiting editors, to whom Eden thought it prudent to accord an interview. And, in case the reader has forgotten it, the Conference on Korea was still making no progress but occupying much time.

Eden enjoyed keeping so many balls in the air at once. He had always liked to spend his days talking to people, reserving the study of official papers until late at night. At Geneva he became less bureaucratic than ever. 'Business within the British delegation was mostly conducted in a levée in Mr Eden's bedroom, on the terrace while sun-bathing, in the drawing-room while he was arranging the flowers, anywhere except in an office round a table'.[13] If it was a strain on his health – those sitting behind him at afternoon sessions would see the back of his neck flushed scarlet – he was surmounting it.

By the middle of May four plenary sessions had drawn out the lines of battle and allowed all concerned ample scope for rhetoric. Working relationships, however intricate and indirect, had been established behind the scenes. Agreement to go into restricted session could reasonably be regarded as the prelude to serious negotiations, as the real starting-point for the Conference.

Then, on the morning of Saturday 15 May – crisis usually comes at the weekend – Eden opened the Swiss newspapers to discover that his allies were in a state of fugue. The French Government, it appeared, had asked the United States what American conditions for military intervention in Indochina would be. Discussions would shortly begin in Paris, where Dulles would meet Laniel.

As a tripartite meeting had already been arranged for that morning, the startled Eden asked first Bedell Smith, who denied all knowledge, then Bidault, who was evasive, for confirmation. When the meeting was over, Bidault asked Eden to talk to Margerie, who revealed enough for Eden to pay a further visit (armed with the European edition of the *New York Herald Tribune* as the ostensible source of his information) on Bedell Smith. He, Eden reported, was 'really distressed' (well he might have been), exploded with indignation at Washington's inability to keep a secret and, in strict confidence, showed Eden the telegrams he himself had received from Washington.[14]

The French and American accounts, even when supplemented by a report from Makins and further conversations with Bidault and Margerie, did not altogether agree, but the story which emerged was serious and disconcerting, more serious than Eden admitted in his memoirs.[15] Simultaneous approaches had been made by Laniel to the US Ambassador in Paris and by the French Ambassador in Washington to Dulles. On 11 May Dulles had telegraphed American conditions for intervention to Dillon in Paris, but the Ambassador had waited to be sure Laniel would survive his vote of confidence before delivering them on 14 May.

There had to be a formal request from the French Government with the endorsement of the National Assembly.

This request must also be addressed to other countries,

including Britain, but British participation (to Laniel's satisfaction) was no longer a sine qua non.[16]

The French must agree to maintain (increase in the French version) their forces in Indochina.

Arrangements for command and training had to be agreed by all the participants.

There must (French version) be an unequivocal declaration of intent to grant full independence to the Associated States, including the right to secede from the French Union.[17]

From the British point of view this was a repetition of the April crisis: less bad because Britain herself was no longer under direct pressure to take military action; worse because three weeks' advocacy of a negotiated settlement had clearly made no impression on French and Americans; worse still, though Eden does not seem to have admitted this, because Bedell Smith had shown himself as slippery as Dulles. Although premature publicity had temporarily defused the grenade of intervention, (Dulles cancelled the press conference called for 19 May)[18] Eden foresaw difficulty in persuading Molotov and Chou en Lai that either Americans or French were seriously interested in negotiations. Commonwealth representatives in Geneva and Commonwealth governments in Asia had to be reassured that Britain was not involved in this Franco-American intrigue and, on 17 May, Churchill again told the House of Commons that Her Majesty's Government 'have not embarked on any negotiation involving commitments'.[19] On the 20th he confirmed that Britain had not been told in advance what her allies were up to.[20]

Eden, described by Bedell Smith as 'quite irritated',[21] commented calmly enough on Sunday 16 May: 'Of course, this American plan will fail like all the others'.[22]

In retrospect one wonders whether it was ever meant to succeed. Margerie did not think a French government could agree to match American reinforcements or to offer the right of secession from the French Union (even Pham van Dong was ready to talk about the French Union).[23] Did Dulles believe Laniel's precarious government could extract such concessions from the National Assembly? Why was the intrigue revealed to the American press (whose stories were published on 14 May) before the US Ambassador in Paris had even delivered the American reply to Laniel?

Bidault, supposed in the French version to have been

uninformed of Laniel's activities, told Eden on 17 May that the French Government did want a negotiated settlement and would not seek American intervention before there had been a demonstrable failure at Geneva. Against this risk, however, they did need insurance and, even while negotiating, the threat of American armed intervention was the only card they had to play.[24]

It is, however, unlikely that either the French or the Americans consistently regarded their intrigues as no more than a bluff, what Denis Allen called 'thunder off'. Margerie, for instance, said that the Americans had been talking in terms of two to three Marine Divisions.[25] Dulles, for his part, had provided a rationalisation for American military intervention as early as the 'terrible dinner' of 1 May. The purpose would be, relying on the precedent of Korea, to hold a bridgehead in Vietnam long enough, say 2 years, for the Americans to train those 300 000 Vietnamese who were supposed to be longing to fight Communists.[26] To satisfy Congress this would have to be part of 'united action' and Dulles may have thought a French request of the kind envisaged would pass muster, even without British support.

One wonders how he reckoned popular opposition in the United States. The Gallup Poll figures of Americans against sending US ground troops to Indochina were rising: by 13 June they reached 72 per cent.[27] Bedell Smith had insisted Eisenhower could alter this overnight,[28] but so far Eisenhower had not tried. Perhaps the explanation lay in Eisenhower's complaint, on 8 June, that French requests for help were always for help on France's own terms.[29] American altruism was never quite so self-effacing.

So was *The Times* needlessly apocalyptic in talking about 'the most dangerous crisis since the end of the world war'? Probably, but there was one American condition for intervention not known to the editor or to Eden, nor disclosed to Laniel. In the words of the United States Joint Chiefs of Staff on 20 May: 'atomic weapons will be used whenever it is to our military advantage'.[30]

7 Restricted Sessions: Restricted Results

'British believe, either honestly or for political effect, that they can continue to play the part of mediator.'—BEDELL SMITH[1]

In a handsomely carpeted room, less spacious than those used for plenary sessions, but still the size of a small house, nine separate tables had been arranged to form a hollow square. At each table sat a delegate, flanked by his principal adviser and his interpreter. Two or three more advisers occupied chairs behind. Along the wall under the windows was a comfortable bench well upholstered in the kind of pale, gleaming, café au lait leather to be found in a Rolls-Royce. There several delegations had installed a junior diplomat to take notes, for the Secretariat of the United Nations were excluded from restricted sessions and each delegation had to make its own record and provide its own interpreter.

Some of these interpreters attracted as much attention as the delegates themselves. Three were Russian, of whom the undoubted star was Prince Andronikof of the French delegation. He had a difficult task, for the French delegates, Chauvel above all, found it hard to interrupt the spontaneous torrent of their own eloquence. Andronikof would listen patiently, making an occasional note, for ten, fifteen, even twenty minutes before he was given the chance to begin a translation that always seemed to combine total recall with elegance and accuracy. I took my own notes while the Frenchman spoke and checked them as Andronikof translated and never found the interpreter in error.

Other delegates were more considerate to their interpreters, though Gromyko, when he appeared instead of Molotov, could not always resist the temptation to correct Troyanovsky's English. His own had a harsh American accent. The Vietminh interpreter had the easiest time of all. Pham van Dong, a man of striking, if ravaged and fanatical appearance, very different from

80

his present plumpness, wrote out his own speeches in French. These he translated into Vietnamese, viva voce, as he delivered them. Then he passed the text to his so-called interpreter, whose command of French was greatly inferior to that of Pham van Dong, to read out. This eccentric practice had the unfortunate result of persuading the delegation of the State of Vietnam, hitherto content to do business in admirable French, that they too should display nationalist fervour by speaking Vietnamese.

Mercifully speeches were shorter than in plenary and some delegates content for their own interpreter to whisper a simultaneous translation. If every speech had been followed by consecutive translation into all the official languages of the Conference, the proceedings would have been still more long-winded. As it was, they were neither brisk nor business-like. To begin with I made copious notes, only to waste much time after the session had ended condensing them into a telegram. Next I curtailed my notes and then I took none, instead drafting the telegram as I listened. Two, three, even four hours of talk could often be accommodated on two sides of a sheet of paper.

At the time the transition to restricted sessions was seen as a great step forward, particularly by those diplomats privileged to be present when others were not, but the extent of the change could be exaggerated. As early as 19 May Molotov complained that most of what had been said in the first two restricted sessions had since appeared in the press.[2] Spokesmen might no longer hold open press conferences, but nor were they inactive. Moreover, when some advance was registered in restricted session, this was usually no more than the ratification of a bargain struck behind the scenes. Exchanges among the nine small tables were still of a debating rather than a negotiating character and strained the patience of some delegates. Also on 19 May Bedell Smith had to be dissuaded by Bidault and Eden from calling for a plenary session at which he could expose the blocking tactics of the other side. Bidault told him that would bring down the French Government.[3] To Washington Bedell Smith reported that the duration of the Conference depended, at least in part, on how long 'British believe, either honestly or for political effect, that they can continue to play the role of mediator.'[4] On 21 May it was Bidault's turn to threaten a call for a return to plenary sessions,[5] but Eden managed to avert the danger until 3 June, when even Molotov became impatient and a plenary session was agreed for the 8th.[6]

In retrospect one can see that the limping progress of the Conference and the impatience this aroused were not really part of anyone's sinister plot, though the Americans were not alone in believing the Communists to be marking time at Geneva so that Vietminh soldiers might gain ground in Indochina. Everybody was having to feel his way. As earlier mentioned, some of the delegations and the governments they represented were uncertain of even their own objectives. On both sides, moreover, participants wondered whether their adversaries really wanted a negotiated settlement at all and, if so, whether there existed any mutually acceptable basis for settlement. Only gradually did it become apparent that the kernel of any settlement – the cessation of hostilities – would have to be negotiated between the two parties who had been doing the fighting: the French and the Vietminh. The task of the Conference was to create a framework for these negotiations: one which would not only encourage the reluctant pair to begin, but which could be regarded by the Americans as a tolerable alternative to widening the war.

This was not what most participants wanted, at least initially. For many months the intermittent attraction of Geneva to the French had sprung from the hope it offered them of avoiding bilateral negotiations – from a position of weakness – with the Vietminh. Ho Chi Minh, however, had been the first to propose such talks and nothing had happened in the following five months to diminish the confidence of the Vietminh in the strength of their hand: at the table or in the field. The argument put forward a quarter of a century later by the Foreign Ministry in Hanoi was probably pressed by Pham van Dong on Molotov and Chou en Lai at Geneva in 1954: 'It is obvious that after Dien Bien Phu, with the assistance of the socialist camp, especially of China, the army and people of Vietnam were capable of liberating their entire country.'[7]

'The assistance of the socialist camp' was even more important to Pham van Dong than 'united action' to Dulles, but 'compromise' must have seemed an equally dirty word to them both.

For Eden and Molotov the key to compromise was partition. The British evolution of this idea has already been described, but Zhivotoski of the Soviet Embassy in London was only the first, on 18 March,[8] of a succession of Soviet diplomats hinting that it would also be acceptable in Moscow. The French had repeatedly and even publicly assured *their* Vietnamese that partition was not a French objective,[9] but the French press had been talking about it since at least the beginning of May[10] and on 7 June the Chief of the Imperial General Staff, after a visit to Paris, reported that Ely and the French military were coming round to the idea.[11] The American military advisers at Geneva – admittedly led by the Admiral Davis who had earlier likened the idea of American intervention to going over Niagara in a barrel[12] – considered partition the only solution as early as 14 May.[13] But for that wild man, Admiral Radford, the military, as often happens, were less bellicose than the civilians. But the British Ambassador in Paris supported on 29 May the view earlier expressed by Bidault: the present French Government could not accept partition and survive.[14] That was one promise they meant to keep.

Eden was nevertheless concerned to establish that the principle of partition should not apply to Cambodia and Laos. His objective, and that of his allies, was to persuade the Conference that the problems of these two countries differed fundamentally from those of Vietnam and could be simply solved by the withdrawal of Vietminh forces and any indigenous supporters they might have recruited. The Communists, of whom Pham van Dong and probably Chou en Lai still regretted Molotov's failure to insist on Khmer Issarak and Pathet Lao representation at Geneva, were not disposed to accept the Royal Governments in Cambodia and Laos as the only expression of popular aspirations in those countries or formal independence from France as a sufficient measure of political change. As for the neutralisation of Cambodia and Laos, which Eden saw both as intrinsically desirable and as an appropriate compensation for their separate treatment, this proved to be not altogether within his gift. Even at the outset the idea encountered reservations from Americans and French as well as Cambodians and Laotians. For weeks repeated discussion of Cambodia and Laos in restricted and plenary sessions brought no progress and even private contacts offered no hope of escape from the impasse.

An equally controversial issue was how the implementation of any eventual agreement or agreements should be supervised. Chou en Lai told the restricted session of 22 May that all delegations appeared to accept that there should be a cease-fire in all the countries of Indochina supervised by a neutral nations commission and guaranteed by the participants in the

Conference.[15] The misleading impression of consensus thus conveyed hid many differences on points of detail, of which one was crucial: the composition of the supervisory commission. Eden wanted a commission capable of producing at least a majority verdict on any contentious issue. Without the backing of a plausibly neutral judgement, it might well be hard to convince non-Communist public opinion that any agreement had been so violated as to require the intervention of the guarantor powers. A supervisory commission of the kind advocated by the Communist delegates – comprising representatives of two Communist (Poland and Czechoslovakia were suggested) and two non-Communist states – could be expected to register deadlock on every issue of any importance. The existence of such a commission would neither deter the Vietminh from violating an agreement nor encourage anyone else to exert themselves in reaction to such a violation.

Eden accordingly proposed – and went on proposing – that the Colombo Powers, an uneven number of neutral and Asian countries, should provide the members of the supervisory commission. He had some warrant for his choice. On 18 May he had summed up the results of his diligent exchanges with these governments and was able to claim a positive response from four out of five:

> *Ceylon* was ready to consider associating herself with an acceptable settlement in Indochina;
> *Pakistan* would consider joining in a guarantee of such a settlement;
> *India* might participate in the work of supervision or even send troops to help implement such a settlement;
> *Burma* would participate in supervision.[16]

This was a confidential assessment for his colleagues in London. On 22 May, in a telegram to Makins, Eden went further: ultimately India, Pakistan and Ceylon might be able to provide the local military backing for a settlement. The British objective should thus be a settlement that drew a line and created a modus vivendi. Her Majesty's Government would not be prepared to participate in the alternative apparently contemplated by the Americans: an organisation that would assist them to reconquer Indochina.[17]

1. Opening session: The Soviet and British delegations are in the foreground: Gromyko, Molotov, Troyanovsky, Allen, Eden and Reading in the front row. The author, laughing, is at right, rear.

Salle des Assemblées

Bibliothèque

Secrétariat

Salle du Conseil

3. Georges Bidault and the pipe-smoking Jean Chauvel.

4. Pham van Dong (on the left).

5. Eden's villa.

8. Dulles, Churchill, Eisenhower, and Eden at the White House in June 1954.

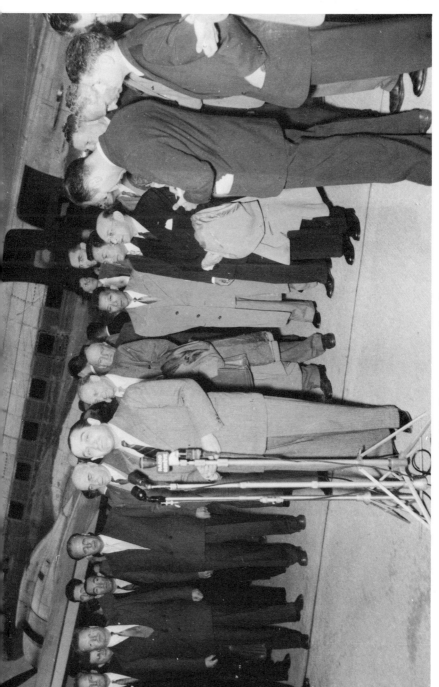

7. Mendès France reaches Geneva.

8. Les Ormeaux: scene of the final drama.

Whether or not the Communist delegates at Geneva had any inkling of Eden's optimistic expectations, they were unwilling to accept the two assumptions on which his arguments obviously rested: that no Communist could ever be neutral, but that some non-Communists could. The second of these notions can scarcely have been more welcome to the Americans – Dulles considered neutrality immoral – but Bedell Smith, presumably confident the Communists would never agree, accepted the Colombo Powers as potential supervisors on 3 June.[18] Bidault, however, could not make up his mind.

His behaviour had become increasingly unpredictable and even embarrassing. At the restricted session of 24 May he was truculent;[19] the next day he puzzled Eden and Bedell Smith by arguing that a seemingly innocuous Communist proposal – that the cease-fire in all three states of Indochina should be simultaneous – was damaging to French prestige.[20] His own delegation explained that he was not in good health. His nerves were badly on edge and he was distracted by worry about the precarious survival of the French Government, about the military situation in Indochina and about the progress of discussions with the United States Government of options in the event of failure at Geneva. On 27 May he was indecisive but agitated and the British Ambassador in Paris suggested he might not 'be thoroughly conscious of what he is doing'.[21] At his first meeting on 1 June with Chou en Lai Bidault was not, in Chauvel's words, 'at his best' and Chou was puzzled.[22] The Chinese press then began to denounce the Laniel Government, and Bidault in particular, for adopting a two-faced attitude, while expressing cautious sympathy for the French Opposition, notably Mendès France.[23] From time to time, too, Soviet diplomats at Geneva would comment to their Western colleagues on Bidault's habit of dropping off to sleep in mid-session. Was he, they would enquire solicitously, quite well? Bedell Smith was blunter on 16 June, after the fall of the Laniel Government, but before the replacement of Bidault. He was 'much the worse for wear'.[24]

Eden could be forgiven if he occasionally found his allies even more trying than his adversaries. When one expects the worst, there is always a chance of being pleasantly surprised. Ultimately that was to happen with Chou en Lai, but, at their first meeting (at a luncheon given by Molotov on 30 April) Eden found Chou inaccessible and rough; hard, cold and bitterly anti-American.[25]

To his staff, however, Eden admitted that Chou was a *large* animal.[26]

That was scarcely surprising. Chou en Lai impressed most people who met him. Malraux found in his early career the inspiration for that remarkable novel *La Condition Humaine*. Field Marshal Montgomery thought him the right man to go into the jungle with and Kissinger's memoirs described Chou with greater admiration and warmth than they accorded to any American statesman.

Chou en Lai was born in 1898, eight years later than Molotov but of a rather better family. Although he did not go to prison until 1919, having by then completed his education in Japan as well as in China, his political experience was both varied and, beyond any reckoning of Eden's, harsh: in France during the early twenties; in all the turbulence of China thereafter; in the civil war; in negotiations with the Kuomintang and in the Long March of the Communist Party into their mountain fastness. He had been Prime Minister and Minister for Foreign Affairs ever since the Communist victory of 1949. His future career would be almost as troubled as Molotov's, but ultimately much more successful.

In 1954 he impressed Chauvel by his intelligence, education, incisiveness and good manners.[27] Trevelyan, the hitherto unrecognised British Chargé d'Affaires in Peking, who met Chou for the first time in Geneva, considered him 'by any standards a remarkable man . . . an extremely adroit negotiator . . . of . . . immense energy and an astonishing capacity for work'. He had great charm and vitality and was always completely at ease.[28] These good qualities, his readiness to give Anglo-Chinese relations a slightly more official character notwithstanding, would not be fully apparent to the British until a later stage of the Conference. Meanwhile it had to be admitted that Chou en Lai, partly by virtue of his physical appearance (those eyebrows not least), was one of the more impressive participants.

Real progress towards eventual agreement was at last recorded on 29 May when the Conference in restricted session agreed that representatives of the French and Vietminh military commands should meet to discuss 'the dispositions of forces to be made upon the cessation of hostilities, beginning with the question of regrouping areas in Vietnam'.[29] This was not, on the face of it, a particularly sensational achievement. Representatives of the two commands had met as early as 19 May – admittedly only to discuss the wounded prisoners from Dien Bien Phu – and the new task now envisaged was rather vaguely defined. But this decision by the Conference not only started the main negotiation: it also began the process of restoring to France the diplomatic manoeuvrability which Bidault had forfeited.

If the agreement of 29 May was important, its achievement was correspondingly difficult, even painful, though it began smoothly enough. When Molotov visited Eden on 25 May to propose the establishment of direct contacts between the two military commands, Eden was able not merely to agree but to give Molotov a draft cleared by officials from the non-Communist delegations of the terms of reference for such bilateral talks. This Molotov welcomed and promised to discuss with the Chinese and Vietminh.

Unfortunately and, considering the vague brevity of the final text, surprisingly, the wording of the terms of reference proved to be a controversial issue, not merely between East and West, but within each of the two groups. It was not resolved in private contacts, nor during the restricted session of 27 May, nor at the meeting of officials of the nine delegations on 28 May. This last was nevertheless noteworthy, because Lord Reading presided – one of the few occasions when he was given a significant job to do. Late that evening Eden put another draft to Molotov and began the restricted session of 29 May with the assumption that this had been generally accepted.

Whether or not Eden's confidence had originally been well-founded – a point on which the documents offer an ambiguous verdict – it was soon shown to be misplaced. Pham Van Dong objected vigorously that the Vietminh could not possibly produce a military representative by the date suggested; the Cambodians had some reservations and Bedell Smith had more. Although agreement was finally reached, the acrimonious session left Eden 'exhausted and not very pleased with what should have been a relatively happy day'.[30]

He would have been even less pleased if he had been able to read the report Bedell Smith telegraphed to Dulles:

Both Eden and Reading gave a startling public exhibition of impatience and pique . . . his performance and that of Lord Reading was absolutely shocking to me . . . their attempt to distort and deceive was so obvious that even Molotov could not swallow it, and his final proposal was, by comparison, reasonable and moderate.[31]

There is naturally no confirmation in the British documents of this harsh account – at most a hint that the last-minute clearing of drafts with non-Communist delegations (the Vietminh were Molotov's responsibility) might have been less than rigorous. Nor do the surviving British participants recollect anything so sensational. Sir Donald Maitland, then Reading's Private Secretary, is sure he would have remembered anything so completely out of character as the behaviour attributed to Lord Reading.[32] Eden, of course, was notorious for his displays of temperament (Bedell Smith had on another occasion remarked to Dulles 'you know how pettish both Eden and Churchill can be at times'),[33] but his outbursts were usually directed towards his own staff or at least took place in private. Chauvel, who was well aware of this reputation of Eden's, nevertheless recorded: 'pour ses partenaires étrangers, il avait the best conference table manners que j'ai vues'.[34] What is clear, however, is that American resentment of Eden and of the British policy Eden directed was by no means confined to Dulles.

All through May, of course, the Americans had continued their efforts to reach agreement with the French on the conditions for intervention in Indochina. The American General Trapnell saw Ely on 27 and 30 May and Laniel on the 31st, but the only result was a decision that Ely (still haunted by the fear of Chinese air intervention) should go to Washington.[35] Dulles continued to complain about Eden and the American press to give prominence to Anglo-US rifts and to criticism of the British policy of appeasement. The Munich analogy became threadbare with daily use. *The Times* of 24 May published a report from their Washington correspondent that mutual distrust and a real American bitterness over Eden's allegedly broken promises now characterised Anglo-American relations.

That was also the day when Eden told the Cabinet (he had spent the weekend at Chequers) that the Americans were unwise in thinking this the moment to challenge China. The Chinese were in no mood to be browbeaten. The Russians wanted a negotiated settlement at Geneva, but the Chinese were not wholly under Russian control, nor were the Vietminh under Chinese control. Nevertheless he believed there was a fair chance of securing agreement at Geneva in two or three weeks time, provided that the Americans could meanwhile be dissuaded from taking unilateral action to intervene militarily (the most dangerous course) in Indochina, to organise their own South East Asian security organisation, or to appeal from Geneva to the United Nations. In the British view the United Nations, from which China was excluded at American insistence, was a forum so objectionable to the Communists that this third course of action meant the rejection of negotiation in favour of a military solution.

The Cabinet agreed that Eden should persevere for a week or two longer.[36] They could hardly have done less. Outside the United States there was little public dissent from Eden's policy. French popular sympathy could be inferred from the successful celebration in Paris of the fiftieth anniversary of the Etente Cordiale. The Australian Government (whose backing was often claimed by Dulles) told all their Missions abroad that they had *not* agreed to the internationalisation of military operations in Indochina but thought the Geneva Conference should be given a chance.[37] In the House of Commons, where Geneva, Indochina and South East Asia had been magnets for parliamentary questions all through May, there was no disposition to attack British policy, only a constant demand for reassurance that it would not be changed. Admittedly this emanated from the Labour Party and, for that reason and from fear of further exacerbating Anglo-American relations, most questions received evasive answers, though Churchill was forthright enough on 20 May in his denial of British prior knowledge of Franco-American intrigues.[38]

As for the British press, not just the loyal *Times*, their praise was becoming embarrassing. On 21 May the left wing weekly *Tribune* had a headline 'EDEN SPEAKS FOR BRITAIN' and their rival, *The New Statesman and Nation*, followed the next day with 'MR. EDEN'S LONE HAND AGAINST ODDS.' Richard Crossman, already a well known Labour politician and later to become a Cabinet Minister, described Eden as the only statesman at Geneva seriously trying to prevent the Indochina incident from turning into a general war. A less welcome comment in the same number was that 'Anthony Eden is now emerging as the new darling of the Labour Left'. It was scarcely surprising to find the next week's issue complaining of those Tories who suspected Eden of preparing a Far Eastern Munich.

They did exist and Eden, who never for a moment forgot his ambition to succeed Churchill, was acutely sensitive to their views. Even Nutting, then Parliamentary Under-Secretary of State for Foreign Affairs and well disposed to Eden, wrote a careful letter to Reading on 23 May suggesting that it would be advisable, even while avoiding any immediate commitment, to express greater public sympathy for American ideas about the organisation of South East Asian defence.[39]

Unfortunately the United States Government were not ready to be soothed by such palliatives. It had taken them until 25 May to accept (after wary scrutiny and amendment) Eden's proposal of 5 May for discussions by the Five Power Staff Agency.[40] When these started in Washington during the first week of June, they caused more distress in Britain than satisfaction in the United States. As Chauvel put it on 1 June, Dulles was like a man who had been bitten by a mosquito: determined upon action of some kind. As he told the Senate on 4 June, the effort to organise collective defence was still going on. What this meant was spelled out that same day to the British Chief of the Imperial General Staff by Admiral Radford: military intervention in Indochina was essential, even at the cost of war with China, who would not, in any case, be backed by Russia. Partition would not do.[41]

8 Phoenix from the Ashes

'If the different positions remained as they were today, then it would be the duty of the Conference to admit to the world its failure.'—EDEN, 10 June 1954[1]

The guarded optimism which the agreement of 29 May had inspired even in the Soviet press, who were echoed by the Chinese in praising Eden's 'policy of understanding',[2] barely survived the end of the month. On 3 June impatience began to spill over. Molotov, who had returned from Moscow the day before, requested a plenary session (the first since 14 May) for 8 June.[3] Bedell Smith reported Eden as believing the impasse on supervision might prove a breaking issue.[4] *The Times* betrayed pessimism. No progress was made in the restricted sessions of 2, 3 and 4 June or in three meetings of military representatives from the two commands.[5]

On 5 June Eden told the Cabinet in London that the chances of securing a favourable outcome at Geneva were not good, largely because the French were so uncertain and hesitant. The Laniel Government were unlikely to last long and whoever succeeded them would want peace at any price. The Americans did not want a successful outcome at Geneva; they were only interested in military intervention. But Dulles envisaged American intervention only as a response to that of the Chinese and Eden believed the Chinese had no intention of intervening.

Eden expressed concern that circumstances had compelled him to adopt the rôle of intermediary between East and West at Geneva and apprehension lest his position might be misrepresented. As it had been misrepresented in the American press (and by Dulles and even Bedell Smith) for many weeks, it is likely that Eden was mainly concerned with British public opinion, particularly in the Conservative party. Churchill responded robustly: 'the chance of preserving world peace should

91

not be prejudiced by irrational American inhibitions against making any contact with Communist representatives'.

A greater danger, Eden argued, was that the negotiations might be fruitlessly prolonged while the Communists improved their military position in Indochina.[6]

This was a genuine source of anxiety at the time – Eden reverted to it in a telegram to Churchill on 15 June[7] – but the logic of the argument is somewhat obscure. There is naturally no dispute about the weakness of the French military position. Navarre, so the Embassy in Paris reported on 26 May, considered it precarious, particularly in the Delta.[8] He expected the Vietminh to be ready to attack by mid-June.[9] Generals Ely and Salan, on their return from a tour of inspection, recommended a shortening of lines in the Delta, the replacement of Navarre and the despatch of reinforcements (for which purpose legislation was needed to allow conscripts to be sent). On 2 June the War Office in London calculated that the Vietminh had a total striking force of 132 mobile battalions (plus 170 static battalions) against a French Union strength of 57 and 185 respectively. It is not surprising that the Legation in Saigon (who had been instructed to telegraph a daily assessment) reported on 4 June that General Cogny, then in command, doubted his ability to hold Hanoi if the Vietminh attacked before the end of June.

All that is puzzling is why anyone should have thought that the French would be worse off militarily if talks continued at Geneva. Today it seems rather more likely that the collapse of the Conference would have precipitated a Vietminh offensive, which might well have succeeded before either French or American reinforcements – assuming both governments were able to overcome the political obstacles to sending them – could have reached Indochina. One suspects that contemporary anxiety was not based on any rigorous analysis of the military situation in Indochina, but was prompted by thoughts of the personal and political embarrassment that the coincidence of talks in Geneva and a major offensive in Indochina would cause. The worst that actually happened was a three-battalion attack on 4 June.[10]

At Geneva there was greater cause for concern. On 7 June Chauvel complained that the Vietminh military representatives were spinning out talks and playing for time, while the Chinese and Russians were now unhelpful.[11] On 8, 9 and 10 June the plenary session demanded by Molotov gave him the opportunity to denounce the United States, France and Bao Dai. Chou en Lai and Pham Van Dong followed suit and Chou was particularly discouraging on the issue of supervision. A neutral nation, he argued, was one which had not taken part in the fighting and the Korean precedent offered no grounds for objecting to the idea that a commission composed of two communists and two non-communists should take only unanimous decisions. On 10 June Eden told the Conference that divergences – on separate treatment for Cambodia and Laos and on international supervision – were wide and deep. 'We have no choice but to resolve them or admit our failure'.[12]

Curiously enough Eden had come close to admitting it already. On 8 June – the first day of the plenary session – Kirkpatrick, acting on instructions, told the United States Ambassador in London that Eden thought agreement at Geneva most unlikely. An attempt should be made to bring the Conference to a close within the next week or ten days. Eden was now disposed to move more rapidly in the formation of a collective defence for South East Asia. The next day Eden telegraphed to Churchill that, failing any Communist concession, it would be necessary to break up the Conference and to encourage Cambodia and Laos to appeal to the United Nations.[13] When Bedell Smith, who had received personal instructions from Eisenhower, urged Eden on 12 June to end the Conference and prepare for intervention,[14] he seemed to be pushing at an open door. What had happened to Eden?

At the time, to the author at least, it seemed a failure of nerve. There was never any question of Eden supposing that an appeal to the United Nations could offer an alternative road to agreement. In the fifties the Chinese Government could rely on other Communist governments to support them in rejecting the United Nations as a source of international legitimacy, even as an appropriate forum for discussions, as long as the seat allotted to China by the Charter was occupied by representatives of the so-called Nationalist government in Taipei. Eden knew that as well as anyone else. An appeal to the United Nations might be used to produce a pretext for military intervention or it could have been just an empty gesture. When Siam, at American instigation, later proposed to the Security Council an investigation of Communist aggression in Indochina, this was promptly vetoed by the Soviet Union on 18 June.[15] Either way the course of action suggested in Eden's telegram of 9 June meant abandoning the policy he had pursued since the end of March.

It is scarcely surprising to find no mention of this episode in Eden's memoirs, only the sensible, but historically disingenuous comment: 'in negotiations of this character, long periods of deadlock are worth enduring while there is any chance that informal talks can uncover fresh possibilities of agreement'.[16] In fact less than a week separated the agreement of 29 May from Eden's gloomy report to the Cabinet on 5 June. Of course, Eden had for many weeks been under constant pressure from the United States Government and their representatives. The sustained criticism of the American press was not only fully and regularly reported to him by the Embassy, but extensively quoted in the British newspapers he read every day. He was aware of uneasiness in the Conservative party and even among certain members of his own staff at the marked deterioration in Anglo-American relations. He had been well supported by Churchill, but the backing of an aged Prime Minister he wanted above all to succeed (Churchill suggested on 11 June that he might retire in September)[17] was no longer enough. On 10 June Eden's junior Ministers at the Foreign Office, Selwyn Lloyd, Nutting and Dodds Parker, endorsed his view that the time had come to break up the Conference. At Geneva, the French, whom he was endeavouring to save in spite of themselves, had been consistently fickle and vacillating. Even Chou and Molotov, hitherto apparently disposed to compromise, had withdrawn into intransigence, leaving Eden out on a limb.

His reaction was understandable – when allies and supporters and even adversaries cannot pick up the step, the leader has at least to consider changing it – but over-hasty. Already on 10 June the Vietminh military representative had proposed to his French interlocutor a secret meeting between the two of them – without, that is to say, the knowledge of any officer from the State of Vietnam. The French, as the British were informed, agreed. The next day, so Bidault told Eden, the Vietminh representative suggested that, if the French were to abandon Tonkin, satisfactory arrangements could probably be made for the rest of Vietnam.[18] Even as the American press were declaring their satisfaction at Eden's speech of 10 June, the basis for eventual agreement had been proposed: the partition of Vietnam, previously rejected by French and Vietnamese alike. On 14 June came Molotov's first concession, to be followed, as we shall see, by more in the rest of the week. Once again, what had happened?

On 9 June the National Assembly in Paris had voted against the Laniel Government, who decided to seek a vote of confidence, lost it on 12 June and resigned on the 13th. In a message to the governments of Burma, Ceylon, India, Pakistan and Siam on 18 June Eden suggested as one explanation for the altered attitude of the Communist delegations that their earlier toughness had now achieved its object: bringing down the Laniel Government.[19] This seems plausible enough: Molotov's demand for a plenary session on his return from Moscow on 3 June coincided with the opening of the Chinese press campaign against the Laniel Government and the marked change of tone in the Soviet press. And the Communists had been given (as had Eden himself) repeated cause to believe that no agreement was possible at Geneva as long as Laniel and Bidault determined French decisions. That conviction, perhaps reinforced by what the Communists did and said at Geneva in the first ten days of June, was one of the reasons why a majority of the National Assembly voted against the government on 12 June.

It is also a more convincing explanation than Eden's alternative suggestion: that the Communists had been influenced by the Western reaction to their own intransigence. Except for Eden, whose public warning that he might be prepared to abandon the Conference came only on 10 June, the Western reaction had in fact been somewhat muted. Eisenhower again expounded his 'domino theory' to a press conference on 7 June,[20] but Dulles admitted the next day that 'united action' had attracted insufficient support to justify an approach to Congress[21] and Eisenhower said on 10 June that he did not intend to seek Congressional authority for intervention in Indochina.[22] *The Times* on 12 June gave the first place to a speech by Dulles complaining of Eden's breach of his April promise. The same newspaper had earlier attributed to Dulles the belief that the British had veto powers over United States policy; the Indians over British; the Chinese over Indian and the Russians over Chinese. So the Russians could veto anything the United States wanted to do! Western disagreements being more conspicuous than any show of resolution, it is scarcely surprising that Bidault, himself only functioning until a new government replaced him, told the French Ambassador in Washington on 15 June that the threat of American intervention was having little effect as a bargaining counter.[23] Dulles had earlier cried Wolf! too often and on this occasion did not even attempt it. Eden was on his own.

Indeed, if the sputtering in the frying pan had been disagreeable, Eden was lucky he did not have to test the temperature of the fire. The policy of the United States at this juncture was not easy for foreigners to understand or follow. The French request for two US Marine Divisions in Indochina had, as Bedell Smith told Eden on 9 June, been refused,[24] although the US Ambassador in Paris thought they were needed if France was to continue the fight.[25] Eisenhower, as we have seen, blamed the French for wanting American help only on their own terms.[26] But the Ambassador, in a burst of impatient candour on 14 June, told Dulles of his own conclusion that 'the chances of US responding favorably to French request even after they have met all conditions are approximately nil'. He thought the course least damaging to NATO and the defence of Western Europe would be to tell the French so.[27] Yet on 16 June Eisenhower wrote to President Coty that the United States were ready to plan new discussions about the united defence of Indochina. The letter was delivered on the 18th,[28] the day after Dulles told the National Security Council in Washington that the French were 'desperately anxious to get themselves out of Indochina . . . probably best to let them quit'.[29]

At Geneva the importance of the approach made to the French by the Vietminh military representative does not seem at first to have been appreciated in the British delegation, perhaps because the move was overshadowed by the fall of the French Government. It was nevertheless doubly significant: that the Vietminh should make such a proposal and that the French should agree to keep it secret from *their* Vietnamese. Twenty years later Kissinger's secret talks in Paris with the North Vietnamese would provide an intriguing parallel.

There was more reason, however, to look Molotov's gift horse in the mouth on 14 June. In that day's restricted session he suggested that the Indian chairman of a four-nation supervisory commission might be given a casting vote to permit majority decisions on questions *not* concerning violations or threatened violations liable to lead to the re-opening of hostilities. The snags were more obvious than the fact that movement had begun.[30] It continued on 15 June (the day the Korean Conference was brought to an end and that the text of Eden's speech of 10 June failed to appease Opposition MPs anxious lest a similar fate should befall the Indochina Conference). Molotov called on Eden to suggest adding Indonesia to his previous list of Czechoslovakia, Poland, India and Pakistan in order to make a five-nation commission. Eden said he would consider the idea, but preferred Burma. He did not tell Molotov that, by coincidence, he had just received a telegram from Rangoon conveying Burmese readiness to take part in supervision and a Burmese warning that Indonesia, being excessively vulnerable to Communist pressure, was the least neutral of the Colombo Powers.

Eden was still suspicious of Molotov's motives in offering concessions, but by now the French were pressing him not to interrupt the Conference. They hoped to reply to the secret Vietminh offer by the end of the week and added that the Chinese had suggested a technical committee to study the proposals so far made on the issue of supervision.

The breakthrough came on 16 June. In restricted session Chou en Lai conceded that 'the situation was not the same in all three states of Indochina' and, while arguing that there really were resistance movements in Laos and Cambodia (the famous Pathet Lao and Khmer Issarak who had been excluded from the Conference), agreed that the question of the withdrawal of foreign troops was the one to be considered. He was even ready to envisage the right of Laos and Cambodia to import arms, provided that foreign bases in these countries were forbidden. After some polemics Pham van Dong seemed prepared, not very graciously, to acquiesce in Chou's proposals, which were endorsed by Molotov and welcomed by Chauvel and Bedell Smith.

When Chou, at his own request, later visited Eden to expand on his ideas, Eden concluded:

It really looks as if the Chinese may want a settlement in Laos and Cambodia: Chou went so far as to say that the Vietminh would respect the unity and independence of Laos and Cambodia and that the Chinese would recognise the Royal Governments, who might be members of the French Union, provided they could be left as free countries without American or other bases.

Chou drew a distinction between Cambodia, where there were only small resistance forces, and Laos, where it would be necessary to establish regrouping areas (as already envisaged for Vietnam). Eden welcomed Chou's remarks and suggested he should repeat them to the French, which Chou agreed to do.[31]

A quarter of a century later the Vietnamese Foreign Ministry in Hanoi complained that China took advantage of her position as the principal supplier of arms to the Vietminh 'to act as the principal negotiator with the French imperialists, and colluding with the latter, to work out a solution advantageous to China and France, but not to the peoples of Vietnam, Laos and Cambodia'.[32] On 17 June, the Ministry's account continues, Chou en Lai made fundamental concessions to Bidault detrimental to the interests of Vietnam.[33] Historically this is inaccurate. Chou's first approach was made to the British, not to the politically paralysed French, and, when he saw Bidault on the 17th, he did not, as the Ministry suggest, concede the principle of two administrations in Vietnam, which Bidault would, in any case, have been personally unwilling to accept and, because of the fall of his government, unable to. Doubtless the Ministry would maintain the 'objective truth' of their account, arguing that Chou must be assumed always to have intended that to which he finally agreed. We lack the other side of the story. Apart from a blanket denial of these allegations by a former Vietnamese Ambassador to China who later settled in Peking:[34] 'Aucun ouvrage d'histoire n'a jamais été produit en Chine populaire qui se rapporte, de près ou de loin, à l'attitude du gouvernement de Pékin sur la question d'Indochine en 1954.'[35]

Molotov, for his part, complemented Chou's concessions on Cambodia and Laos by repeating in the restricted session his proposal for a fifth member of the International Commission or, if this was preferred, a three-nation commission comprising India (as chairman), Poland and Indonesia, or some other Asian country.

The next day was one for catching up. Chauvel, who had earlier expressed to Harold Caccia the view that France should come to terms at once, told Bedell Smith and Eden he had persuaded Bidault to agree 'that the top secret military conversations between the French and Vietminh delegations which had hitherto been proceeding on a purely personal and unofficial basis should now be regarded as official'. Ely, who had been consulted on the Vietminh proposal of 11 June, favoured bargaining French evacuation of the Delta against the removal of the Vietminh from South Vietnam, though Bidault still found it difficult to face the prospect of partition.

Bedell Smith expressed the hope that the French would nevertheless manage to hold on to Haiphong (the main northern port). In reporting this to London Eden, whose suspicions had come full circle in the last 48 hours, assumed that the Americans wanted Haiphong as a bridgehead for their eventual reconquest of Indochina.

Chauvel was also able to say that he hoped to make progress in private talks with the Chinese, Cambodians and Laotians. In a few days it should be possible for the Foreign Ministers to leave the work of the Conference in the hands of their deputies. The French, though Chauvel did not say so, were obviously regaining the leading rôle which should always have been theirs. Even Bidault, who had been the main impediment, was able to report that his talks with Molotov and Chou en Lai had given him the impression they were anxious to reach agreement.

June 17 was Bidault's last day as French Foreign Minister and Eden's parting comment crystallised his rôle in our story: 'Bidault . . . is in a strange mood these days and alternates brief bouts of realism with brave speeches about his future as Prime Minister of France and how his country will yet recover everything including Indochina.'[36]

Bidault did again become Prime Minister, briefly in April 1958, but he was soon caught up in the death throes of French Algeria and the birth pangs of the Fifth Republic. As one of the leaders of French resistance to General de Gaulle he spent much of the Sixties in exile. He died, in 1983, a disappointed man.

After a last angry gesture on 18 June from the United States delegation – the fanatical Walter Robertson appearing in the restricted session instead of Bedell Smith to reject the Chinese proposals the latter had welcomed on the 16th – the Conference agreed on 19 June to match the military talks on the cessation of hostilities in Vietnam with similar discussions concerning Cambodia and Laos. 'The representatives of the Commands of the two sides' were told to 'study the questions relating to the cessation of hostilities . . . beginning with the question concerning the withdrawal of all foreign forces and of foreign military personnel, due regard being had to the observations and proposals presented by the various delegations at the Conference'.

It was a loosely formulated compromise solution to a singularly contentious issue – adopted in that form partly because some of the delegates were in a hurry.[37]

Eden, in particular, wanted to absent himself from Geneva because he was due to fly to Washington with Churchill on 24 June. This Anglo-American meeting had been brewing for a long time – Dulles found the idea premature on 9 May[38] – and had been prompted partly by Churchill's perpetual eagerness for such encounters, partly by an understandable desire to attempt a little fence-mending. When Churchill told the Cabinet on 5 June of Eisenhower's agreement, Eden was torn between reluctance to leave Geneva and determination that Churchill should not go alone.[39] That dilemma was resolved by a slight postponement of the Washington meeting and the acceleration of proceedings at Geneva.

A change of government made an interlude equally convenient to the French; the State Department were happy to be able to tell the rump of their delegation 'to take no substantive positions except those pursuant to specific instructions',[40] and the rest of the delegations probably accepted that they would have little to do before some progress had been made in the three sets of military talks. The Vietminh, incidentally, had not responded when told on 17 June that the French were now ready to discuss their secret proposal. Perhaps they wanted first to form some idea of the character of the new French Government.

Eden urged both Molotov and Chou en Lai, when they came to say goodbye on 19 June, not to expect greater concessions from the new French Government than they would have demanded of its predecessor. He also asked Chou to restrain the Vietminh from launching any military attacks in Indochina and, when he later learned that Chou would be visiting Nehru during his absence from Geneva, sent Nehru a personal message requesting him to say the same to Chou and also to urge the importance of separate treatment for Cambodia and Laos. Molotov, for his part, expressed the hope that Eden, during his visit to Washington, might be able to persuade the Americans to alter their negative stance towards the Conference. He had never understood Bidault's attitude[41] (Chou said much the same that day to a Canadian visitor)[42] but hoped for better things from his successor. He and Eden agreed that the Conference had at least relaxed international tension.

On 20 June Eden, Bedell Smith and Molotov left Geneva for their respective capitals, leaving rump delegations in the charge of subordinates. Chauvel, the 57 year old professional diplomat who had now, to the great relief of most delegations, come into his own, stayed. So did Chou en Lai, who had some last tasks to perform before he started on his travels. The Conference, of which Eden had briefly despaired, had survived to wrangle another month.

9   France Takes the Lead

'Mendès France fought his corner brilliantly and I am more than ever convinced that for the first time since we have resumed office we have a Frenchman who knows what he wants and will fight for it.'—EDEN, 14 July 1954[1]

Pierre Mendès France, born into a Jewish family in 1907 and thus the youngest of the leading actors in our story, began his political career in 1932 as the youngest deputy elected (he was 25), but was serving in the air force when refusal to accept French capitulation led to his arrest by the Vichy régime in 1940. He continued his political career after his escape and a further spell in the air force, this time that of the Free French, who then entrusted him with important administrative responsibilities. The war once over his advancement languished a little and, compared with Bidault's string of ministerial offices, he had no prizes to display. This did not stop the British Embassy in Paris, in June 1953 when Mendès France was a Radical deputy backed by the newspaper *L'Express*, from nominating him as the man best able to save France.[2] But his bid for the premiership (won, curiously enough, by a politician equally lacking in experience of major office – Joseph Laniel) failed by 13 votes.

His opposition to French policy in Indochina, which he had first expressed in 1950 and had reiterated in the speech that proclaimed his candidature for the premiership, was then too much for a predominantly right-wing assembly to stomach. As the war in Indochina – and the Laniel government which could hold out no hope of ending that war – grew increasingly unpopular, Mendès France came to be regarded, both at home and abroad, as the leading figure of the opposition. In Britain he was personally little known (though the Embassy kept in touch and one of their counsellors – Tony Rumbold – was now Eden's Private Secretary) and in the United States he was suspected of left-wing views. In both countries his reputation suffered a little from the constant efforts of the Laniel government to persuade the British and Americans that 'après nous, le déluge'.

There was, of course, no stable or coherent majority to support that government and from the moment of its formation its fall had been only a matter of time, just as mere chance would determine the occasion for that fall. Laniel himself blamed the European Defence Community rather than Indochina for his overthrow,[3] but his government had repeatedly been endangered by suspicions of its lack of enthusiasm for a negotiated settlement at Geneva and it was this that Mendès France seized on when the government was defeated in the second week of June 1954.

Having been invited on 13 June by the President of the Republic to form a government, Mendès France not merely proclaimed as his first objective a cease-fire in Indochina within a month, but, when soliciting the Assembly's support on the 17th, gave an audacious undertaking:

Je me présenterai devant vous avant le 20 juillet et je vous rendrai compte des résultats obtenus. Si aucune solution satisfaisante n'a pu aboutir à cette date . . . mon gouvernement remettra sa démission à M. le président de la République.

He thereby risked more than his own reputation. His country's adversaries might be tempted to protract negotiations in the hope of extracting last-minute concessions as the deadline of 20 July drew near.

No less boldly, but also prudently, Mendès France then declared he would only form a government if he received enough votes from the Assembly to constitute a majority *without* counting the Communists. After he had got his majority (419 to 47 on 18 June) and formed a government in which he decided to be his own Foreign Minister,[4] he eventually went back to the Assembly on 7 July, reiterated his promise to resign if there was no prospect by 20 July of a cease-fire, but added that, before resigning, he would ask the Assembly (Gladwyn Jebb thought they would never agree) to authorise the despatch of conscripts to Indochina.[5] The British Embassy had been right, a year earlier, in attributing to Mendès France a dislike of half-measures.[6]

Between those two dates much had happened. One event attracted less British attention than it deserved: Ngo Dinh Diem became Prime Minister of the State of Vietnam (a post he would retain, with the title changed to President of the Republic, until his assassination in 1963) on the same 18th of June 1954 that raised Mendès France to the premiership of France. Only Bedell Smith was enthusiastic[7] and gave Mendès France no encouragement when the latter requested, on 20 June, a restraining American influence on this 'fanatic much like Synghman Rhee'[8] (the difficult dictator of South Korea). The United States Embassy in Paris, however, had earlier called Diem a 'Yogi-like mystic'[9] and the Chargé d'Affaires in Saigon thought him 'a messiah without a message'.[10] The British Legation in Saigon reported that Bao Dai's appeal to the Vietnamese people to support Diem had attracted little notice, but that there was a reasonable turnout at the airport when he arrived on 26 June.[11]

British attention was focused on Mendès France. Eden lunched with him in Paris on 20 June on his way back from Geneva to London. In response to a request for advice Eden urged him to accept the proposal made by Chou en Lai for an early meeting. When Mendès France so decided and, later that afternoon, told Bedell Smith, the latter was not pleased, but said he could make no formal objection. Mendès France, who did not take to Bedell Smith, that evening charged Gladwyn Jebb with a cordial message for Eden,[12] who was himself impressed by the 'intensive driving power and ruthlessness' of Mendès France.[13] That impression was obviously the basis of Churchill's personal message to Eisenhower the following day: 'personally I think Mendès France, whom I do not know, has made up his mind to clear out on the best terms available. If that is so, I think he is right'.[14]

Eden's most immediate business was naturally at home. On 22 June he told the Cabinet (still more concerned that month with Egypt than with Indochina) that a negotiated settlement was 'not beyond reach' (perhaps double negatives were a personal preference) and must not be jeopardised by ostentatious haste in the proclamation of arrangements for collective defence in South East Asia. In Washington he and Churchill would have to persuade the Americans accordingly and to convince them that there could be no British commitment to 'united action' until after Geneva.[15]

The next day Eden made his report to the House of Commons. For him this was a major political opportunity and he spoke not only as Foreign Secretary, but as a politician, tacitly as a would-be prime minister. Read today the speech seems a reasonable, rather bland account of the Geneva Conference and its antecedents. At the time there were obviously audible overtones of that earlier headline in the *New Statesman* 'MR EDEN'S LONE HAND AGAINST ODDS'. This went down well at Westminster – Harold Macmillan, a good judge as well as a rival, commented: 'Eden's position in the country is higher than it has ever been'[16] – but not in the United States (in France they liked the speech). Makins reported American press reaction as ranging from cool to critical. The speech was 'bristling with criticism of the United States' and, worse still, this drew cheers from both Conservatives and Labour. Eden had managed to pay tribute to the cooperation he had received from all the leading actors, whom he named – except Dulles. And the Locarno suggestion, to which we must return, was 'poison to Americans'.[17]

Mendès France was meanwhile picking his way more cautiously, acutely conscious of his vulnerability to charges (not only in the American press) that his policy was one of surrender. His meeting with Chou en Lai, for instance, had to take place in the French Embassy at Berne: going to Geneva would have made Mendès France seem a suppliant. Their conversation lasted two hours and was cordial, though Mendès France admitted that Chou was more relaxed than he was: 'l'homme était impressionant'.[18]

Chou said the first essential was an armistice in all three countries of Indochina, followed by elections in Vietnam for the reunification of that country under a single government. If the representatives of the various military commands were so instructed, they could reach agreement on the terms of cease-fire in three weeks, when the Foreign Ministers could return to Geneva. Mendès France was less than delighted to hear, on 23 June, of the time-table thus envisaged by Chou. The latter added – and this disquieted Eden when he read the full account communicated to him by the French – that the Royal Governments of Cambodia and Laos should talk to the resistance movements in those countries (Pathet Lao and Khmer Issarak riding again?) with a view to arranging elections there as well.

Mendès France agreed, as Chou had insisted, that there should be no American bases in Cambodia or Laos. He also accepted the principle of elections in Vietnam, but argued that these could not be held immediately and he expressed his concern that the

Vietminh were seeking a temporary partition line unreasonably far to the south. Chou suggested a personal talk with Pham van Dong, but Mendès France, mentioning the difficulties of his political position, said he would have to think about that. Chou, who had previously talked to the Cambodians and Laotians at Geneva and put them in touch with the Vietminh delegation, then left for China via Delhi and Rangoon. Mendès France returned to Paris.

At Geneva matters were not going quite as smoothly as the encouraging tone adopted by Chou might have suggested. Admittedly Chauvel was able to have a reasonably amicable meeting with Pham Van Dong on 22 June – in Chou's villa at Le Grand Mont-Fleuri, which he put at their disposal for this and subsequent meetings. But, by the end of the month, the French were offering 18°N as the temporary partition line in Vietnam and the Vietminh still demanding 13°N. This was in the military talks at Geneva. The parallel discussions which, by the terms of the Conference decision of 29 May, were to be held in Tongking, had not got off the ground because of Vietminh objections to the participation of Vietnamese officers. The French evidently thought they could get away with excluding their clients at Geneva, but not in Vietnam itself.[19] As late as 9 July the Vietminh (at Geneva) had reduced their bid only to 14°N, though the French seemed by then also to have abandoned their optimistic demand for an enclave at Haiphong.

Talks about Laos and Cambodia did not really get going until 4 July, when the Vietminh had to make concessions: on reference to the Pathet Lao in the first case and, in the second, by accepting the Cambodians as the only other party to the agreement. The Vietminh had wanted French representatives to be included in these talks, but found the Cambodians stubbornly opposed.[20] It was one of the first indications of the trouble Cambodian intransigence would cause at Geneva as well as in Indochina itself.

The slow progress of bilateral talks was not compensated by any faster tempo in the Conference itself. While the Foreign Ministers were away (only Pham Van Dong stayed in Geneva) half a dozen restricted sessions were held, mainly concerned with supervision, but none of them registered any advance. The British Delegation were probably not alone in having instructions not to reach agreement in their master's absence, but they were unique in being led by someone so junior as a Counsellor. Lord Reading, who had been left in charge when Eden departed, taking 20 members of the delegation with him, stayed only until 24 June. Thereafter Tahourdin headed the delegation, though Sir Lionel Lamb, the Ambassador at Berne, came over when there was a restricted session to lend dignity to the occasion and match the presence of such high-ranking figures as Chauvel, the Vice-Ministers Li Konung and Kuznetsov and, of course, Pham Van Dong. Although the down-grading of the British Delegation drew complaints from French and Americans, it can have done little harm.[21]

As Lamb wrote to Reading on 7 July, Chauvel was the only active and constructive participant in this phase of the Conference. The Communist representatives were stalling and using their speeches to attack the Americans. The Russians, however, were exerting themselves to display friendship for the British and he instanced a dinner given by Kuznetsov for the delegation the night before. Tahourdin, who wrote separately, described the atmosphere of the party as 'very cordial',[22] a notable under-statement, for this was still the period when Russians habitually tried (the practice has not been entirely abandoned even today) to make their guests drunk with constant toasts in vodka – 'bottoms up'. Having swallowed a precautionary bumper of olive oil before leaving the hotel, I was fortunate enough to survive and to enjoy my first experience of *caviare aux blinis*.

Stagnation at Geneva was not, contrary to Eden's earlier apprehensions, accompanied by any major recrudescence of military activity in Indochina, though there was skirmishing and both sides accused the other of provocative conduct. The French, however, had taken significant precautions. A brigade group was sent to Indochina by sea on 15 June. As usual, this was much less than the British thought necessary (Sir John Harding, the CIGS, put the requirement at two to three divisions and 300 aircraft), but the three new divisions Ely was forming (for North Africa as well as Indochina) included conscripts and could not be sent without the passage of special legislation. On 1 July, therefore, the evacuation of French and Vietnamese troops, together with many thousands of civilians, from much of the Delta was begun. By 5 July, when *The Times* reported the news as being a shock to delegates in Geneva, the withdrawal had been successfully completed and French Union forces now held only a salient, based on the sea and embracing the cities of Hanoi and Haiphong. Ngo Dinh Diem, himself a northerner, was indignant, but the desertion rate in the Vietnamese army scarcely allowed him to put forward any alternative.[23]

Options other than a negotiated settlement were becoming harder and harder to discern. Bedell Smith had confided to Casey (who passed it on to Eden) on 17 June that intervention with American forces was now *out*.[24] Churchill, in a personal message of 21 June to Eisenhower, declared:

> In no foreseeable circumstances, except possibly a local rescue, could British troops be used in Indochina, and if we were asked our opinion we should advise against US local intervention except for rescue.[25]

As for the French, whatever Mendès France might say in public or Ely plan in secret, the prospect that a successor government would undertake a renewed campaign did not exist. The alternative to compromise was scuttle.

Unfortunately, as we have previously noted, there is a great gulf between the intellectual and the political acceptance of unwelcome truth and nowhere was that gulf wider than in Washington. Bedell Smith might now have come round to the view expressed on 26 May by the prescient Mr Ogburn, Regional Planning Adviser in the Bureau of Far Eastern Affairs: 'I can find no honest grounds on which the sending of American troops to Indochina . . . could be justified'.[26] That did not mean that Eden would find it any easier to convince Dulles of the need for a negotiated settlement. And, after the collapse of so many previous ideas, a new one had just surfaced in Washington, where the Policy Planning Staff had proposed that the United States should join forces with Cambodia, Laos and Vietnam to break up the Geneva Conference and should then give them armed assistance.[27] Dulles had written off the French, sending a message to President Coty that earlier American discussions with Laniel should be regarded as having lapsed. As he told Eden on 26 June, the US Government wanted to wipe the slate clean.[28]

When Churchill and Eden set out on 24 June, they knew nothing of the Planners' notions, but they were well aware that their task would not be easy. Feelings in Washington were more sensitive than usual. It was not, after all, only British policy that had come under the constant lash of the United States press: so had American. Soon the influential Alsop brothers would write that British policy, if one of surrender, was at least coherent, whereas that of the United States was in a condition of near bankruptcy.[29] *The Times* on 18 June had quoted their Washington correspondent for the view that differences between the two governments 'are deeper than anyone would like to admit in public'. It was not entirely on account of Indochina. The two governments had never seen eye to eye on Egypt. The much publicised antics of Senator McCarthy continued to make an unfortunate impression on British public opinion. And now there was Guatemala, whose left wing government were endeavouring to import arms, some of them in British ships, for use against the incursion of a resistance movement, allegedly organised by the US Central Intelligence Agency, from across the frontier. In Geneva, where the problem seemed familiar, some diplomats wondered whether the rebels should be called Pathet Guatemala or, alternatively, Guatemala Issarak.

These were not speculations Eden could afford. The French might now be making the running at Geneva, but the British still had to clear the field for them in Washington. The ideal composition envisaged by Eden was naturally a triptych of allies united by their sober determination to negotiate an acceptable settlement. But even the spectacle, so distressing to British public opinion, of a rabid United States barely restrained by Britain and France from open belligerence would have a better effect at Geneva than the opposite picture of Americans aloofly washing their hands of the problems of feckless allies. The need for thunder off had not diminished, but it was now harder, in the last act, to make it sound credible.

Mendès France had much the same idea. On 26 June a French aide-mémoire was delivered to Eden and Dulles emphasising the importance, if an acceptable agreement was to be reached at Geneva, of maintaining Communist apprehensions that intransigence on their part might lead to wider conflict. The expedient suggested was the inclusion in any communiqué issued after the Anglo-American talks of a statement to the effect that failure to reach a reasonable agreement would aggravate international tension. The aide-mémoire also repeated the request earlier made by Mendès France that American influence should be employed to moderate the indignant hostility to be expected from Ngo Dinh Diem.

Before Eden and Dulles were ready to tackle French problems they had first to address themselves to their own. A start was made on 25 June by setting up a joint study group to consider how Britain and the United States might associate themselves with any acceptable agreement reached at Geneva; what kind of collective security pact should be established in South East Asia; and what should be done if no agreement were reached at Geneva.[30] This was an earnest of Eden's intention to honour, at the appropriate moment, his undertaking of 13 April. Churchill, moreover, had told Eisenhower on 21 June in the same message that rejected British military intervention in Indochina: 'we should certainly have a SEATO'[31] [South East Asia Treaty Organisation]. Then Eden had to explain his reference to Locarno, such a curious cause of Anglo-American friction that the reader also deserves some explanation.

In 1925, when Eden was young and Churchill in vigorous middle age, seven treaties were initialled at Locarno, of which the most important guaranteed the German-Belgian and German-French frontiers, committing both Britain and Italy to go to war if France attacked Germany or Germany France. The enthusiastic reception of this treaty in Britain (the then Foreign Secretary was created a Knight of the Garter) seems to have made an impression on Churchill and Eden that easily survived the failure of the Locarno system at its first test: Hitler's invasion of the Rhineland in 1936. The analogy had been present to Eden's mind since the beginning of the Geneva Conference, Churchill had mentioned it in the House of Commons on 11 May and, in his speech of 23 June, Eden said: 'I hope we shall be able to agree to an international guarantee of any settlement that may emerge at Geneva . . . a reciprocal arrangement in which both sides take part, such as Locarno'.[32]

Eden in his memoirs hints that some of the American indignation aroused by this reference may have originated in confusion between Locarno and Munich, but this was naturally not true of Dulles. Nor was Eden's comment – 'after our talks, I was satisfied that the American administration not only understood what it meant, but seemed to like the idea' – [33]true of Dulles. He told Eden bluntly on 26 June that the idea would amount to expressing moral approval of a Communist success and was therefore unacceptable. The most the United States Government could do would be to say it would not use force to upset an agreement on Indochina, a suggestion Eden had perforce to welcome, but which had nothing to do with the Locarno precedent.[34] That was one of the ideas which Eden, as sometimes happened when he was face to face with Dulles, had to drop. On 30 June the House of Representatives rubbed home American hostility to Locarno by resolving to withhold aid from governments committed by treaty to maintain Communist rule over any defined area in Asia.

On 28 June, however, the joint communiqué issued by Eisenhower and Churchill contained a passage which amply met, as he himself later acknowledged, the requirements of Mendès France:

> We discussed South East Asia and, in particular, examined the situation which would arise from the conclusion of an agreement on Indochina. We also considered the situation which would arise from failure to reach such an agreement. We will press forward with plans for collective defence to meet either eventuality. We are both convinced that if at Geneva the French Government is confronted with demands which prevent an acceptable agreement regarding Indochina, the international situation will be seriously aggravated.[35]

The vague menace of this communiqué was distinctly more cost-effective than the attempted precision of the Seven Points (see Appendix 1) drawn up the following day by Dulles and Eden (whose advisers on this ocasion included Harold Caccia and Denis Allen). This confidential document specified the kind of Indochina agreement which the two powers could accept and was also intended for communication to the French Government. The communiqué was at once read by Mendès France, whereas the British and American aide-mémoires embodying the Seven Points got side-tracked in the Quai d'Orsay. When Mendès France did see them, he was puzzled by their ambiguity and quite missed the subtle significance of the difference Dulles had devised in the circumstances of their delivery. The British Ambassador in Paris, when handing over the aide-mémoire, made an oral offer of diplomatic support at Geneva, a gesture which the moral principles of Mr Dulles made it impossible for the United States

Ambassador to imitate. Several days passed before anyone explained this to Mendès France.

Briefly, however, the Seven Points provided that an acceptable agreement should preserve the integrity of Laos and Cambodia, at least the southern half of Vietnam and, if possible, an enclave in the Delta. It should not restrict the possibility of maintaining non-communist régimes in Indochina and it should provide for effective international supervision.[36] The internal contradictions of this document and the extent to which its provisions were reflected in the agreement eventually reached at Geneva will be considered in the next chapter.

Of course Indochina was only one item on the Washington agenda. *The Times* commented that much more time was spent by Churchill and Eisenhower on Western Europe than on South East Asia and that the former subject commanded greater agreement. There was also Egypt and a windy declaration modelled on the Atlantic Charter of 1941. Although some of the wording slightly worried the Cabinet (as had that of its predecessor) the name coined by *The Times* – Potomac Charter – did not catch on and the declaration made little impact on events or the memories of men. Some rapprochement between the two governments, even over South East Asia, there had nevertheless been, though Denis Allen's comment on 1 July – 'the American attitude seems to be becoming a little bit more flexible' –[37] was probably nearer the mark than Churchill's later statement to the House of Commons that the Washington talks had 'helped to get Anglo-American discussion of the problems of South East Asia back on to a realistic and constructive level'.[38]

The press on both sides of the Atlantic, the loyal *Times* always excepted, struck a sharper note. *Time Magazine* described Eden as 'busily courting the Communists' and hinted he was thinking of maintaining a neutral posture between the United States and the Soviet Union. *Tribune* produced on 2 July the headline: 'DID CHURCHILL CAVE IN?' The *New Statesman* was more optimistic: the Americans had been 'prevented from actually cutting the ground from under the feet of M Mendès France', but a somewhat critical anxiety coloured many of the parliamentary questions asked in the first fortnight of July. And, in private, Dulles condemned the British on 4 July 'for efforts to conclude peace at any price'.[39] This was a little unfair: since Eden left Geneva on 20 June and lunched with Mendès France on the way home, there had been no serious

British discussions with anyone except the Americans. Dulles might have made some concessions in the Washington talks, but he remained sour and suspicious.

This became obvious on 7 July, when he sent a message to Eden saying he was not at present in favour either of returning to Geneva himself or of sending Bedell Smith.[40] This was awkward. Mendès France told Gladwyn Jebb he wanted to be in Geneva, where Molotov was expected on 8 July, as soon as possible, but was anxious that Eden should be there as well. In his reply of the 8th Eden explained that he could not get to Geneva before the 12th. That was also the day chosen by Chou en Lai, as Trevelyan reported from Peking, together with the news that Chou had seen Ho Chi Minh, the leader of the Vietminh, and agreed with him how to settle matters at Geneva.[41] Dulles, however, remained obdurate (he had announced his decision to a press conference on 8 July) in spite of British and French pressure. Eisenhower told him on 10 July that he would like to comply with British and French requests,[42] but Dulles still held out, sending a long message on 12 July to Eden and Mendès France explaining his reluctance to return to Geneva as due to his doubts whether the French were pursuing a policy he could support. Finally, at Eisenhower's insistence, Dulles travelled as far as Paris and, on 13 July, Eden and Mendès France left Geneva to meet him there. Molotov called, by previous arrangement, just before Eden's departure and permitted himself some sarcasm at the expense of Dulles.

Whether Dulles really had to be pushed by Eisenhower or was playing hard to get is not altogether clear. Certainly he arrived in Paris fully prepared to submit Mendès France not merely to a viva, but to a written examination on the various 'position papers' he brought with him. As Eden reported to Churchill, 'Mendès France fought his corner brilliantly' and the sustained argument begun on the afternoon of the 13th eventually resulted in agreement soon after luncheon on the 14th. In exchange for a long letter from Mendès France promising to seek an agreement embodying the Seven Points, Dulles undertook to send Bedell Smith back to Geneva. Eden, for his part, promised to do his best to help Mendès France achieve a settlement. These exchanges were secret, but the communiqué mentioned that Eden had supported the request made by Mendès France for American representation in the Conference at ministerial level and this, according to Gladwyn Jebb, earned Eden shouts of 'merci' from French passers-by as he drove to the airport.

'Dulles', Eden commented, 'cut a sorry figure'.[43] Eden presumably meant that Dulles had failed to get the better of Mendès France, but the remark could also have been applied to the distrust Dulles had publicly manifested of his allies and the pressure he had publicly applied in summoning them to Paris. Dulles, of course, had told the press that Mendès France had invited him to come, but this was only after the US Ambassador in Paris had gone to Geneva to talk Mendès France into it. Perhaps Dulles, who had forgiven and forgotten nothing, might have retorted that written assurances were necessary and so was the method of their extraction. But *The Times* complained on 12 July that the position of Britain and France in the Conference had been weakened by the coldness and suspicion evinced by the United States Government. And Attlee's comments in the foreign affairs debate in the House of Commons were sharp enough to provoke Churchill, on 14 July, into calling Attlee's speech 'one long whine of criticism against the United States'.[44]

At the time Eden seems to have regarded the ministerial representation at Geneva of the United States as well worth all the effort expended in achieving it. He was probably relieved that the actual representative was Bedell Smith rather than Dulles. In retrospect one wonders whether the concessions made by the Communists during the last week of the Conference had not mostly been decided earlier. Would they have been withheld if American alienation had been manifest in the person of Walter Robertson at the head of the United States Delegation rather than implicit in what *The Times*, on 17 July, called the observer status of Bedell Smith? Perhaps his presence was needed, not to overawe Molotov and Chou en Lai, but to save their face, no less than that of Eden and Mendès France.

This is an argument not generally perceived at the time nor, even thirty years later, susceptible of proof. What is still remarkable is the deference Mendès France was willing to display to get Bedell Smith to Geneva. It would not have happened under or after de Gaulle.

10 Last Act

'It is not what we would have liked to have had. But . . . if I have
no better plan I am not going to criticise what they have
done.'—EISENHOWER[1]

As the Conference accelerated towards its close, the conduct of
diplomacy at Geneva took on a novel and somewhat unexpected
character. That it became increasingly hectic was the predictable
result of the deadline set by Mendès France. What was surprising
was that the 9 delegations met only once – on 18 July – before their
final session on 21 July. Serious business was transacted in
bilateral encounters or in the ad hoc meetings of representatives
from three, or four, or five delegations. Nor were the active
participants the same. On 1 June Eden had complained to Bidault
and Bedell Smith that he was becoming ever more embarrassed
by his monopoly of the diplomatic initiative. 'I was continuously
producing proposals, because, if I did not, nothing happened'.[2]
    This was certainly not true of the final phase of the Conference.
On 16 July, when British, French and Soviet experts met to
consider the various drafts so far produced, these had emanated
from the French, Soviet, Vietminh or Cambodian delegations.[3]
The British rôle was to be consulted, to encourage compromise, to
warn against intransigence, to chair a conference that seldom sat:
not to take initiatives on matters of substance. In the discharge of
that responsibility the French continued to take the lead, but, as
we shall see, they were now joined by others. Only the Americans
became entirely responsive and, for the most part, inert.
    The last act began when Mendès France arrived in Geneva on
10 July, visiting Molotov that evening and receiving Pham van
Dong the next day. These encounters brought no movement,
though Mendès France evaded Molotov's attempt to discuss the
European Defence Community and was stirred by the emotional
significance of his first contact with Pham van Dong, who seems
himself to have been somewhat moved. The latter's villa was next

door to Joli-Port, where Mendès France was living, but Pham van Dong found the use of his black Zis limousine for the hundred yard journey more consonant with the dignity of his people.[4] Personal meetings of this kind continued throughout the first few days in spite of the partial interruption caused by the flying visit of Eden and Mendès France to Paris. It was significant that Tran van Do, representing the State of Vietnam, met Pham van Dong on 13 July for the first time since the Conference had begun; that Chou en Lai paid a return call on the Laotian delegation on 14 July and that on the 15th Eden, who had hitherto kept his distance from the lesser fry, was severally visited by the representatives of all three Associated States. Barriers were crumbling and delegates beginning to behave more normally.

In particular, Geneva's most embarrassing anomaly was at last resolved. On 13 July the French disclosed to their Vietnamese allies the existence and the nature of the secret talks they had been conducting for over a month with the Vietminh. This course of action had been strongly urged on the French Government the day before by the United States Ambassador in Paris, who reinforced, as he had been instructed, the impact of his advice by telling the Quai d'Orsay that the attitude of the United States to an Indochina settlement would be much influenced by that of the Associated States. He added that his colleague in Saigon would be telling Ngo Dinh Diem in general terms about the kind of settlement that would be considered acceptable in Washington. Even in London the Foreign Office were disconcerted when told of the American intervention.

Tran van Do, nominally Diem's Foreign Minister, did not take the French revelation too badly, perhaps because he already had some inkling of the truth, perhaps because he was a realist. On 15 July he told Eden that Diem wanted an enclave in the North, but he himself considered the idea hopeless in view of the military situation on the ground.[5] Although he delivered a note on 17 July protesting against everything done by the French at Geneva and demanding that the whole territory of Vietnam should provisionally be placed under the control and protection of the United Nations, this was on instructions from Saigon. So was his formal rejection, at the Restricted Session of 18 July, of the principle of partition. The next day he told Eden his protest had been merely for the record.[6] But all this activity, just because it was so much at variance with the course being taken by the leaders of the Conference, was a warning of trouble to come. At Geneva Tran van Do might complain to Eden, as he did on 13 July, that the treaty granting independence to the State of Vietnam, though initialled by the French long ago, had never been brought into effect.[7] In Saigon Diem, with American encouragement, was beginning to behave as if it had.

Meanwhile, from the three sets of discussions between military representatives of the opposing commands and from a host of bilateral encounters and ad hoc meetings, the shape of an eventual settlement was beginning to emerge. For each of the three countries of Indochina – Cambodia, Laos and Vietnam – there would be a separate agreement on the cessation of hostilities. From Cambodia and Laos all foreign forces would be withdrawn and Laotian insurgents concentrated, pending a political settlement, in two provinces. In Vietnam the opposing forces throughout the country would regroup and, where appropriate, withdraw either side of a single demarcation line: the Vietminh to the north; French Union forces and their Vietnamese allies to the south.

These agreements would be lengthy, detailed and complex, varying considerably from one country to another. Each had to specify the actions that would follow a cease-fire: the disengagement, regrouping or withdrawal of opposing forces; the exchange of prisoners; the avoidance of reprisals; the cessation, with certain qualifications and exceptions, of reinforcement or the introduction of military equipment; the time-limits for these operations and the provisions for their supervision. The drafts had always been lengthy, but it was soon obvious that, on legal or political or diplomatic or even sentimental grounds, for good reasons or for bad, not everything could be accommodated within the three documents. They would have to be supplemented by unilateral declarations from various governments. And the framework, including some important provisions of a political and international character, would be furnished by a Final Declaration from the Geneva Conference as a whole.

By 16 July the drafts and counter-drafts examined by British, French and Soviet officials had reached an advanced stage of preparation and covered much of the ground. But, as Mendès France pointed out to Eden and Molotov that morning, the value of this elaborate diplomatic tapestry was much impaired by three ragged holes in the fabric of the settlement. In Vietnam the entire agreement on the cessation of hostilities flowed from the opening sentence of Article 1: 'a provisional military demarcation line shall be fixed, on either side of which the forces of the two parties shall be regrouped after their withdrawal. . .'. But the French wanted this line to be 18°N and the Vietminh, having yielded much ground since their June demand for 13°N, had now stuck at 16°N. And the Vietminh wanted, as the French did not, a fixed date on which elections would be held for the reunification of Vietnam. Lastly, but for Eden perhaps most importantly, no satisfactory arrangements could be made for supervision of any of the agreements until it had been determined who was to do the supervising.

These were the major problems, but, as John Tahourdin reported later that day, the tripartite meeting of officials managed to identify a dozen issues which only the foreign ministers themselves could resolve.

The next day Chou en Lai tackled first Mendès France, then Eden, about the problem that seemed to be causing him most concern: his fear that the United States and their allies meant Cambodia, Laos and South Vietnam to become members of the projected South East Asia Treaty Organisation (SEATO). If that was the intention, so he told Eden, then the outlook for a settlement at Geneva was not good. Eden replied that he was not aware of any such plan (Mendès France seems to have been more forthright in his denial). Eden went on to argue that the creation of SEATO need cause China no apprehension. It would be a purely defensive alliance. Chou did not agree. He thought SEATO likely to cause as much tension in Asia as had NATO in Europe. He would have much preferred a Locarno-type pact.[8]

On 19 July, having first obtained the agreement of Bedell Smith (who had returned to Geneva on 17 July), Eden sent Harold Caccia to tell Chang Wen-Tien, then the second man in the Chinese delegation, that if, as part of the Geneva Agreements, the Associated States undertook not to join military alliances, then they would not become members of SEATO. The Chinese were not told that the Allies might nevertheless regard their protection as embracing the territory of Cambodia, Laos and South Vietnam, even if these states were not members of the organisation.[9] In practice no British government ever accepted such an obligation, repeated American representations notwithstanding.

Meanwhile 18 July had been an eventful day. Eden began it on a gloomy note by telegraphing to Churchill that there was no more than an even chance of reaching agreement. Remembering that the 20th was the deadline fixed by Mendès France (who had himself found Molotov unyielding at dinner on the 15th) and that tripartite analysis on the 16th revealed fundamental divergences, this was not unduly pessimistic. Since that earlier breakthrough in the third week of June, there had been much progress on points of detail and some reciprocity in concessions, but no gesture large enough to impart to the Conference a confident momentum.

Eden sought a measure of cover against any outcome by sending messages to the governments of Australia and New Zealand and the five Colombo Powers asking them to issue declarations of support for agreements on Indochina, if these were reached at Geneva, or for the security and collective defence of South East Asia, in case there was no agreement. It was optimistic of him to include the Colombo Powers in the light of their likely reactions to an appeal for what would have been at least an implicit military commitment.[10] It was a curious coincidence that he should have done so on the same day as Makins sent a telegram on the subject. The Americans, the Ambassador reported, had derived from the meetings (concluded the day before) of the Joint UK-US Study Group a better understanding of the importance Eden attached to the Colombo Powers. But they still suspected Eden of having fastened on the issue as a pretext for delay. It was still a grudge.[11] For that matter Dulles, who seems to have had little inkling of the new balance of political forces, was that day 'fearful Eden will try to push Mendès France into agreement far short of 7 points'.[12]

On the same afternoon Chou en Lai suddenly suggested to Eden that India, Canada and Poland should provide the members of the supervisory commissions in Cambodia, Laos and Vietnam. This combination of one neutral, one westerner and one communist seemed as obviously responsive to everyone's requirements as it was altogether unexpected. Eden thought Krishna Menon, who had spent the last week flitting from flower to flower in Geneva as an international busybody given privileged status by his personal friendship with Nehru, must have suggested the idea to Chou, perhaps as a way of excluding Pakistan. But Krishna Menon, though never afflicted by modesty, does not seem to have claimed the honour and Chou himself was a man of considerable intelligence, imagination and initiative.

When breaking the news, which he did the same day, to the rest of the Colombo Powers, Eden did not suggest the initiative had been anything but Chinese. Bedell Smith nevertheless found no cause for objection and Mendès France, who initially wondered whether to propose Belgium instead of Canada, agreed the following day. A major hurdle had been removed, though Mendès France was still concerned by the attitude on other issues of Pham Van Dong. The day ended in anti-climax: a restricted session at which the only speakers were Tran van Do (rejecting partition) and Bedell Smith explaining that the United States would not forcibly disturb any settlement they could respect. Eden wondered why on earth Molotov had insisted on having the meeting.

On the evening of 19 July, while the active negotiators were still labouring at their drafts, Eden tackled Molotov about the Final Declaration. Mendès France, whom Bedell Smith had warned of his own inability to sign any final declaration, was worried that the Chinese might insist on an actual signature from every delegation. Eden managed to persuade Molotov that the Final Declaration might be adopted by the Conference orally.

Nevertheless, it was not until 20 July that the crucial issues were resolved. Between them Mendès France and Pham Van Dong agreed that the demarcation line in Vietnam should be on the 17th parallel and the elections in July 1956. These two issues had to be settled together. 17°N gave French Union forces and the Vietnamese troops that would succeed them a short, defensible line as the northern boundary of South Vietnam. It kept more territory and some significant towns out of the clutches of the Vietminh. It was close to the line envisaged in the American Seven Points which Mendès France had accepted as his objective. For these concessions the Vietminh price was a definite date for the elections which would enable them to win politically that southern half of Vietnam which their allies had refused to help them to conquer militarily.

Then, together with Eden and Molotov, the four men agreed on the provisions of the Final Declaration,[13] the document that incorporated the promise of elections in July 1956. Presumably the Chinese, who had still been arguing that morning that everyone should sign, had meanwhile been persuaded by the Russians to change their mind.[14] It was a day of last minute decisions, including one by the Cabinet that Eden should endorse the settlement even if the United States were unwilling formally to accept any agreement.[15]

At 11.19 p.m. on 20 July Eden telegraphed to London that the terms of the agreement on the cessation of hostilities had been agreed for Vietnam and would, he hoped, be agreed for Laos within an hour or two. The Cambodians, however, were giving much trouble.

This disturbing news had been broken to Eden and Molotov by Mendès France some two hours earlier.[16] An ad hoc gathering then assembled at the Villa Les Ormeaux in Prégny, one of Geneva's semi-rural suburbs. This building had throughout the Conference accommodated the offices and communications facilities of the British delegation. In the last phase Eden, who had earlier given up his tenancy of Le Reposoir, also lived at Les Ormeaux. The villa boasted a hall of ample though not baronial dimensions, panelled and furnished in ugly, fretted, uncomfortable pitch-pine. This now served as the scene of the decisive encounter between the Cambodian and Vietminh delegations, with Eden, Molotov and Mendès France playing a mediatory rôle that, particularly in the case of the two last, sometimes assumed an almost coercive character. The three men naturally had their advisers with them and, the arena being where it was, more British officials than were strictly necessary managed to creep into the back row of the stalls for the one genuinely dramatic spectacle of the entire Conference.

It was dramatic because nobody had prepared or rehearsed it. The debate was entirely impromptu and it lasted three hours, easily exceeding the limit set by Mendès France in June. If anyone anywhere, as many writers have suggested, stopped the clocks, this had not been done at Les Ormeaux by the time the meeting ended at two o'clock in the morning of 21 July.

The cause of this drama was Cambodian refusal to conform to the general pattern envisaged by French and Vietminh alike for the three cease-fire agreements in Indochina, particularly the ban (to be found in the Laotian and Vietnamese agreements) on the introduction of reinforcements, armaments or foreign military bases. Chou en Lai and Molotov and Pham van Dong, Eden and Mendès France, even, reluctantly and usually tacitly, Bedell Smith had all regarded such provisions as part of the major international bargain: Cambodia and Laos should be independent provided they were neutralised. Now the Cambodians were rejecting such constraints (which the docile Laotians had accepted and the French imposed on the Vietnamese) because they were incompatible with Cambodian independence and sovereignty. It was not that they *wanted* foreign troops, arms or bases, but that they should not be denied the right to have them if they chose.

If it had not been so serious – a last minute threat to the entire Indochina settlement – the spectacle would have been comic. It even elicited a single, sardonic laugh from Molotov. The Great Men, and the Great Powers, had, in the words later employed by *The Times* 'averted one of the most acute dangers of a great war that the world has faced since 1946', only to find all their achievements jeopardised because Cambodians remembered their French logic but forgot the lines allotted to their part. An American, of course, would have cried 'Munich', but might not have seen the true application of his analogy. For the Czech was Pham van Dong, expostulating in fluent and increasingly embittered French, but under remorseless pressure from Molotov until he conceded the Cambodian demands. A quarter of a century later, as seen from Hanoi, it was 'the Chinese leaders' who 'betrayed the revolutionary struggle of the peoples of Vietnam, Laos and Cambodia',[17] but the Chinese, though they had seen the Cambodians on the morning of 20 July,[18] were not present that night.

Although any apportionment of the responsibility between Chinese and Russians must await access to the archives in Hanoi, Moscow and Peking, it was obvious at the time and has become increasingly so, that the Vietminh were under pressure from their allies. This pressure was latent from the start of the Conference, constrained initially by uncertainty over French intentions, perhaps suspended in case more could be squeezed from Mendès France and his time limit, finally blatant.

Accounts differ as to the times when the three agreements (all dated, to save face for Mendès France, at midnight on 20 July) were actually signed, but the Americans, as detached observers, said 0330 on 21 July for Vietnam and Laos, 1100 for Cambodia,[19] though the British 1245 has the attraction of heightened drama and the added plausibility of being just before luncheon.[20]

At three o'clock that afternoon the Geneva Conference assembled in plenary session, Eden in the chair. There were ten documents for consideration: the three agreements on the cessation of hostilities, each accompanied by two unilateral declarations by, respectively, the Cambodian, Laotian and French governments; and the Final Declaration of the Geneva Conference as a whole. To these were then added an unilateral declaration, of calculated ambiguity, by the representative of the United States; an amendment (which was not accepted) to the Final Declaration from the State of Vietnam; and an oral reservation of Cambodian claims on part of the territory of Vietnam. Mr Tep Phan had no success with this final piece of impudence.

These were the Geneva Agreements, intended at the time and subsequently usually considered to form a single corpus, but so riddled with legal and political anomalies as to offer the participants a wealth of pretexts for the variety of their conflicting interpretations. The three agreements on the cessation of hostilities, for instance, were actually signed by both sides and constituted the nearest approach to proper treaties. But those concerning Laos and Vietnam were signed on behalf of French military commanders. So whom did they bind once French troops had been withdrawn from countries which had become independent? Neither Bao Dai nor Ngo Dinh Diem ever accepted the agreement on Vietnam. The Final Declaration (see Appendix 2) listed all nine members of the Conference in its preamble and, in its detailed provisions, repeatedly referred without qualification to 'the Conference' as if all were unanimous in their solidarity. Yet everyone knew this not to be true of the United States and of the State of Vietnam, even if neither of them actually repudiated the Final Declaration on 21 July 1954.

Legal quibbles apart, the Final Declaration had five main functions. It brought the Conference to a formal end. It emphasised the international importance of the military obligations assumed by those actually involved in the fighting. It outlined the basis of an eventual political settlement. It committed all concerned 'to respect the sovereignty, the independence, the unity and the territorial integrity' of Cambodia, Laos and Vietnam 'and to refrain from interference in their internal affairs'. It imposed, perhaps not on the United States, whose unilateral declaration took note only of Articles 1 to 12, the obligation set out in Article 13 of mutual consultation on issues referred to the Members of the Conference by the

International Supervisory Commissions.[21] These were useful functions and, if they entailed a procedural nonsense, that then seemed the only way to meet conflicting political requirements, to end hostilities in Indochina and to preserve the peace of the world by saving face. Most of those concerned probably permitted themselves at least a secret sigh of relief at the immediate result and, in looking with more or less confidence towards the future, hoped for the best. Even the Vietminh could expect to gain from the 1956 elections what their allies had refused to help them take on the battlefield: the unification of Vietnam under their own rule. And nobody else was eager to continue, let alone start, fighting. If the Geneva Agreements, more than most, hinged on that hidden clause, *rebus sic stantibus*, (as long as political circumstances remain the same) the singularity of their procedure has since often been surpassed, not least in the affairs of Indochina.

Of course, what had been achieved at Geneva was not a final or even an immediate settlement. Fighting ceased in Indochina by instalments from 27 July to the middle of August. There was no equivalent of the 1918 Armistice in which the entire Western Front fell silent at 11 o'clock on the morning of the 11th of November. Up to ten months had been allowed for subsequent military arrangements, the dates envisaged for political solutions were still more distant and no term was assigned to the tasks of the International Supervisory Commissions. What really happened on 21 July was that the nine delegations could go home and at least the British Government could turn their attention to other problems.

At the time the gossip of Geneva attributed the rapid dispersal of the Conference, indeed its successful conclusion, to the knowledge that every hotel room in the city had been reserved for a convention of American dentists. Be that as it may, the British delegation were airborne the same evening after a brief celebration at the buffet so hospitably decked by the United Nations after, or in the interval of, every session of the Conference. On this occasion the customary tea and coffee, the assortment of more potent cordials, the gaseous waters, the canapés and petits fours, had been supplemented by copious champagne. French officers were supposed indignantly to have rejected the Vietminh proposal to toast the signature of the agreements on the cessation of hostilities, but French diplomats now seemed as appreciative as anyone else. Nor did the austere sourness of the distant Dulles seem to be diminishing the consumption of the Americans. The benefits of the United Nations should be enjoyed, as rosebuds are gathered, while they may.

Before this interval of indulgence was reached, the Conference had tacitly acquiesced in a proposal of which nobody then realised the significance. It will be explored in the Epilogue. That proposal was made, with Molotov's agreement, by Eden.

Certain costs arise from the decisions which the Conference has taken. It is suggested that it should be left here to your Chairmen as their parting gift to put before you some proposal in respect of those costs. I only wish to add in that connection that, as this Conference is peculiar in not having any Secretariat in the usual sense of the term, the two Chairmen, with considerable reluctance, are prepared to undertake this highly invidious task. The costs to which I refer are not our own but those of the International Commission.[22]

It would be nearly twenty years before the last repercussions of that innocent proposal died away.

Most people welcomed the Geneva Agreements. That was particularly true of Britain. *The Times* was in ecstasy: 'cause for deep thankfulness . . . ten weeks of unremitting imaginative skill on the part of the British Foreign Secretary . . . clinched by Mendès France . . . arrangement finally reached . . . inevitable . . . better than feared'. Macmillan recorded in his diary: 'far more satisfactory than one could have hoped . . . Eden's prestige and authority will be much increased'.[23] Eden himself told the House of Commons: 'there was a wide danger for us all. So long as the fighting continued there was an ever-present risk that the conflict would spread, with measureless consequences. In so far as our toils have averted these dangers, they have been, I am sure, a real gain for peace'. Congratulations were general and Herbert Morrison, for the Opposition, not only paid tribute to Eden, but imitated him in giving credit to Mendès France as well.[24] Both Churchill[25] and *The Times*, however, thought the response of the Conservative Party had been rather reserved.

In France *The Times* noted 'deep relief', but the debate in the National Assembly, which gave Mendès France a handsome majority, was marred by party feuding. A tribute to Eden was applauded and Mendès France described the agreements as the end of a nightmare for France. If some of their provisions seemed cruel, that was because the facts were cruel. In Indochina French lives need no longer be lost in a futile conflict, but 'l'oeuvre française en Indochine', as the President of the Assembly described it, had been brutally ended.

In the circumstances ambivalence was inevitable. Bidault had prepared a violently hostile speech but, when his turn came, could not be found. It was after dinner. That should have been his last appearance in our story, but he did later speak, only to curtail his remarks in confusion when caught out by Mendès France in factual error.[26]

The Chinese carried enthusiasm furthest. Chou en Lai gave a dinner on 22 July – not everyone had hurried away from Geneva – to Pham van Dong and the representatives of the Associated States. This may have been one of the occasions for which the food was flown in from China. At the dinner Chou proposed the health of Bao Dai and suggested to Diem's brother, who was one of the guests, that the State of Vietnam should open a legation in Peking. Pham van Dong, who had thanked the Co-Chairmen at the final session of the Conference but had not mentioned China or the Soviet Union, was understandably startled. He was probably not alone. Chou himself regarded the Agreements as giving China what she wanted: the exclusion of the Americans from Indochina.[27] At the official celebrations in Peking on 24 July, credit for the agreements, described as a 'setback to the United States', was given to France, the Vietminh, China, the Soviet Union and Britain.[28]

This praise for Britain was not echoed from Moscow, though Molotov had been no less complimentary to Eden at Geneva than had Chou en Lai. *Tass* on 23 July criticised the United States, conceded France had belatedly seen sense, did not mention the rôle of Britain.[29] The official history later said that Eden, being opposed to US military intervention in Vietnam, had 'persuaded Dulles to use more flexible methods'. In a curious echo of American views this British restraint was said to have been 'prompted by the attitude of India'.[30]

Congratulations to Eden flowed in from the Commonwealth, from the Colombo Powers (who took care to give due credit to themselves for the achievement of agreement at Geneva), even from Belgrade. It was not until 3 August, however, that the Colombo Powers, whom Eden had reminded on 24 July, made a collective response to his appeal for a declaration of support for the Geneva Agreements. Then they expressed 'their deep satisfaction at the agreements that have been reached . . . they expect that these agreements will be fully respected'. Neither then, nor in the statements most of the five governments had earlier issued individually, was there any assumption of any kind of commitment, express or implied.[31] It would be surprising if no one in the State Department was stimulated into sardonic comment on the outcome of Eden's 'expense of spirit in a waste of shame'.

In the United States Bedell Smith was almost alone in emulating the magnaminity of Eisenhower's comment quoted at the beginning of this chapter. Bedell Smith, who reached Washington on 23 July, said: 'diplomacy is rarely able to gain at the conference table what cannot be gained or held on the battlefield'. At a press conference on the same day Dulles made it sufficiently clear that *he* did not welcome the agreements[32] and at the end of the month Makins called 'the initial American reaction . . . distinctly sour'.

It was scarcely surprising. The United States Government had never wanted a negotiated settlement and the settlement actually achieved was not entirely compatible with the Seven Points (see Appendix 1) on which Dulles had insisted and to which first Eden and then Mendès France had subscribed. The Communists would not, of course, have accepted an agreement which imposed no restrictions (as suggested by Point 3) on the introduction into South Vietnam of arms and military advisers, but the existence of such restrictions seemed to the Americans deplorable and would ultimately prove embarrassing. On the other hand, what they saw as the major flaw of the settlement – the political provisions for the future of Vietnam – was not merely an essential element in the bargain, but actually reflected the internal contradictions of the Seven Points.

Point 4 rejected 'political provisions which would risk loss of the retained area to communist control', but Point 5 said 'the possibility of the ultimate reunification of Vietnam by peaceful means' must not be excluded. The provision in Article 7 of the Final Declaration for 'free general elections by secret ballot . . . in July 1946 under the supervision of an international commission' met the requirements of the American Point 5, but was clearly incompatible with Point 4. It was unfortunate that American respect for the principles of national reunification and free elections (reflected in their own unilateral declaration) prevented them from saying frankly that elections were impermissible if they might, as most people then believed, be won by the Communists. Nor would Ngo Dinh Diem and the Vietnamese whose support the Americans hoped to win have accepted a declaration that the partition of Vietnam must be political and permanent, as in Germany and Korea, rather than military, brief and provisional.

So the Americans could neither accept nor openly reject the Geneva Settlement. Government, politicians and press could only be sour at what *The New Statesman*, on 24 July, was not alone in considering their 'unmitigated defeat at Geneva'.

As reactions in Indochina itself never excited much interest in London, the last word and a note of perhaps forgivable complacency may be allowed to John Tahourdin, who concluded a summary of the provisions of the Geneva Agreements, submitted on 26 July, with the comment: 'It is substantially what was proposed by the Foreign Office last March, though then brushed aside by the United States Government'.[33]

11 Myths

'Eden's friendly gesture to Attlee also constituted, for good or ill, the final blow to the chances of an *international* anti-Communist intervention in Indochina.'—DAVID CARLTON[1]

Before considering, in the Epilogue, the principal consequences of the 1954 Geneva Settlement and the repercussions of British diplomatic involvement, it may be useful to hack away some of the undergrowth. Strange legends have since encrusted the events surrounding the Conference, the motives of those concerned and the results.

THE CONSPIRACY THEORY

Various people, some of whom should have known better, have argued that the 1954 Geneva Settlement was the price paid by the Soviet Union for French refusal to ratify the treaties establishing the European Defence Community. That there was a connection between these two issues is undoubted, but the evidence places the hinge in Washington rather than Moscow. The Laniel Government had scarcely been formed in July 1953 before they were emphasising that their fall was bound to follow any failure of American financial support for the war in Indochina. The force of their further warning that no other French government would either stay in Indochina or arrange ratification of the European Defence Community was appreciated by the National Security Council in Washington as early as 6 August 1953.[2] On 7 September the US Ambassador in Paris had to dissuade his Government from putting the link between aid for the Indochina war and ratification into writing[3] and, as late as 15 December 1953, the US Chargé d'Affaires in Saigon had to deny that American aid for Indochina was conditional on French ratification of the EDC.[4] In October, however, the Conseil de la

129

République in Paris came out against the whole idea of the EDC, which was again denounced by General de Gaulle on 12 November.[5] A later debate in the National Assembly (which the government survived) revealed growing opposition and the Anglo-American onslaught at the Bermuda Conference at the beginning of December was no more successful than the threat made, in the middle of the month, by Dulles of an 'agonising reappraisal of basic United States policy'.[6] It was not that Laniel and Bidault were personally opposed to French ratification. They just did not think they would get it through and they were sure no other French government would even try.

At Berlin, therefore, it was Dulles, not Molotov, who conceded to Bidault the principle of including Indochina on the agenda of a Five Power Conference at Geneva. To Molotov the Conference, needed to assert the Great Power status of his Chinese allies, was then more important than its agenda. It was Dulles who had to admit to Bidault that 'refusal on the part of the United States or your Government to be willing to talk peace in Indochina would put the principal proponents of the European Defence Community in a most difficult position in France.'[7] The prospect of a negotiated settlement in Indochina was the price paid by the *Americans* for the prospect of French ratification of the EDC.

The opposite hypothesis – that peace in Indochina could only be obtained by abandoning the EDC – was expressly repudiated by Bidault in the National Assembly on 24 February 1954: 'on n'échange pas Adenauer contre Ho Chi Minh'.[8] A mere denial by Bidault might be insufficient if there was any evidence that French ratification of the EDC was ever politically possible; that it could have been perceived by Molotov as a real danger worth paying a substantial price to avert. But it was Dulles, on 3 March, who said he had 'reluctantly accepted the French position with reference to Indochina on basis of assurances that this would facilitate prompt action on EDC'.[9]

Dulles was optimistic. He did not realise that there was no majority for the EDC or, for most Frenchmen, any acceptable alternative to peace in Indochina. On 14 April, just as the wave of crisis there was about to break, Dulles pressed Laniel to announce a date for starting the debate on ratifying the EDC.[10] But the French Government, torn between negotiating a settlement in Indochina and seeking American military intervention, were already teetering on the brink of collapse. They had no desire, probably no capacity, to assume extra political liabilities. On 18 May 1954, when the Laniel Government were experiencing a rush of bellicose blood to the head, it was the US Ambassador in Paris who told his government that the EDC must be considered dead 'if we fail to reach agreement with French for joint, effective and hopeful action in Indochina'.[11]

By the time the Laniel Government fell on 12 June – according to Laniel himself because he was believed to want a debate on the EDC –[12] the prospect of French ratification had never become remotely probable. The Foreign Affairs Committee of the National Assembly voted against it on 9 June.[13] It is inconceivable that the Soviet Ambassador in Paris would ever have reported ratification to be so probable that the Soviet Government should make concessions on Indochina as the only way of avoiding it.

The idea of a Franco-Soviet deal was a winter fantasy – invented in 1953 by politicians and journalists to tease the Laniel Government – that was merely warmed up for Mendès France. Yet, if ratification was not to be feared from Laniel, who had half promised it to the Americans, how could it be expected from Mendès France, who was known to be agnostic? All he said in his investiture speech was that he would introduce 'definite proposals' before mid-August. What these might be was sufficiently indicated by his comment: 'en une matière si délicate, aucune solution ne peut être bonne, admissible même, si elle est imposée par une faible majorité à une minorité ardente; une large adhésion nationale s'impose'.[14] This was eventually given expression by a free vote in the National Assembly, which buried the EDC at the end of August 1954.

The advocates of the conspiracy theory can, of course, believe Mendès France when he says Molotov mentioned the EDC on 10 July 1954, yet not credit his own refusal to discuss the subject.[15] But, if they think the two men reached a bargain, then or at any other time, they must first explain what there was in it for Molotov. On 18 June, the day Mendès France became Prime Minister, the Defence Committee of the National Assembly imitated their colleagues on the Foreign Affairs Committee by voting against ratification of the EDC.[16] As the British Ambassador in Paris, who considered Mendès France as 'difficult but entirely honest', later remarked, the idea of a deal with Molotov was 'inherently absurd'.[17]

There was an equally keen observer, but one who was as passionately committed to the EDC as he was opposed to a negotiated settlement at Geneva; a man never slow to think the worst of his allies nor reluctant to give his thoughts expression. If there had been a Franco-Soviet deal, Dulles would have suspected it and Dulles would have voiced his suspicions – probably at a press conference.

EDEN AND NEHRU

Eden's personal relations with other statesmen have attracted much attention, some of it misconceived. It is strange, for instance, that both Americans and Russians should have attributed Eden's policies to the influence of Nehru and that both should have been wrong. It was not merely that Eden disliked Nehru – 'miserable little Indian Kerensky':[18] what was much more important was that Eden neither understood Nehru nor tried to. Knowing Nehru to be almost as vain as himself, Eden naturally expected that continued flattery would persuade Nehru to support British policies. The existence of distinctive Indian assumptions, interests and objectives was never really present to Eden's mind. The constant solicitations he addressed to Nehru were not merely unduly optimistic: their recipient was a figment of Eden's imagination, one of those Kipling characters whose oriental ambiguity only masks their fundamental soundness.

What Eden never seems to have done was to apply his mind to the messages he received from Nehru and to the reports of the United Kingdom High Commissioner in New Delhi. It was early apparent, for instance, that Nehru did not want to be associated with Pakistan in anything to do with Indochina. Yet Eden went bumbling on about the Colombo Powers until he was rescued by Chou en Lai, who obviously recognised, as Eden did not, that Canada and Poland were, to such a political snob as Nehru, much more suitable countries to supply subordinates to an Indian chairman than the rag-tag-and bobtail of Burma, Ceylon and Indonesia, to say nothing of the obnoxious Pakistan. Eden tried hard, however naïvely and whatever his motives, to influence Nehru. There is no evidence that Nehru influenced him. Americans and Russians asserted an opposite view to explain what both regarded as Eden's unnatural divergence from the policy of the United States.

EDEN AND THE LABOUR PARTY

David Carlton's suggestion that Eden's policy towards Indochina was prompted by his desire to support Attlee, the sober, responsible Leader of the Labour Party, against such left-wing rivals as Aneurin Bevan is one of the flaws produced by an unduly transatlantic orientation in an otherwise admirable biography. Of course Eden preferred Attlee to Bevan: anyone of his background and formation would. But Eden was a Conservative politician intent on becoming a Conservative Prime Minister. In the fifties the Tories needed Aneurin Bevan as much as they needed Tony Benn in the eighties: those were the men who kept them in power. Eden had no interest at all in building up Attlee, an ex-Prime Minister of proved competence, as the respectable figurehead of the Opposition. Moreover, if Eden was temperamental, he was not frivolous. He did not follow controversial and risky policies merely to please Attlee or Nehru any more than he did merely to spite Dulles.

EDEN AND DULLES

This said, it is nevertheless surprising to find Carlton suggesting that the ill-feeling between Eden and Dulles has been exaggerated. One of his arguments – that the two men occasionally exchanged friendly messages[19] – only shows that Carlton has himself never been required to draft such messages. Whatever may have been true of other periods, American as well as British documents demonstrate that before and during the Geneva Conference the two men disliked and distrusted one another. The only interval of relative bonhomie was at Bermuda in December 1953, perhaps as a reaction to the bad temper exhibited by Eisenhower and Churchill. Their strained relations can not be blamed, as Carlton seems to intend, on Eden alone. The French found Dulles equally trying and Eden managed to get on surprisingly well with Bedell Smith, though even the latter's obituarist emphasised how short was the fuse on the General's notorious temper.

The true exaggeration, ever since the unhappy débâcle at Suez in 1956, has been of the strictly diplomatic significance of Eden's temperamental weaknesses. However badly he sometimes behaved to his subordinates – and two of his successors were worse – he seldom gave foreigners cause for complaint and his performance at Geneva drew tributes from all sides. Chauvel has already been cited, but it is worth noting Casey's comment on 'Eden's almost inhuman good humour and patience'.[20]

If these qualities were seldom apparent in his relationship with Dulles, the blame cannot be cast upon Eden alone. Dulles lacked, as even his own biographers testify, an endearing personality. On 13 October 1953, for instance, when Eden had only just returned to the Foreign Office after a long absence, Makins pleaded that the British media should be persuaded to welcome Dulles on his forthcoming visit to London. 'I know he feels very keenly the constant attacks which are made on him from British sources and anything that can be done to make him feel at home would be helpful'. Nutting commented that Salisbury had already talked to diplomatic correspondents during the summer and the News Department said they would do their best, adding 'Dulles is a much maligned character, due largely, as we all know, to his clumsy public performances particularly where press correspondents are concerned'.[21] Obviously Eden was not alone in being more sensitive to his own feelings than to those of others.

In substance, of course, the dispute was one between the British and United States Governments. These had separately considered, in the light of British and American national interests, the attitude they should adopt towards the problem of Indochina and had, with some deliberation and well aware of the different views on the other side of the Atlantic, reached mutually incompatible conclusions. Each had decided the first step should be to convert the other.

In April 1954, after his visit to London, Dulles thought he had succeeded. But Eden, having complied against his will, was of the same opinion still and took the first opportunity, in his Easter outburst, not only of going back on his agreement, but of denying he had agreed at all. The resentment this aroused in Dulles was understandable, but its somewhat repetitive expression – not only by Dulles himself, but by his subordinates – inevitably reinforced in Eden the moral indignation we always feel towards those whom we have injured. The reasonable pursuit of British national interests, as these had authoritatively been defined after more than the usual allowance of discussion, assumed for Eden a specifically anti-American character which worried many of his officials. Unfortunately, his angry and too personal suspicions were constantly given credibility by Dulles himself, who could neither restrain his public loquacity nor keep secret his intrigues with the French. It would be tedious to recapitulate all the acts, of commission or of omission, by which the two men fuelled the process, but distrust and dislike spiralled on both sides of the ocean. It is particularly significant how often these sentiments surface in confidential documents intended by Dulles for American eyes only.

It can well be argued, by those of Tolstoyan inclinations, that this mutual antipathy made little difference to the outcome in 1954. Dulles was going against the grain of history. A better relationship with Eden might have eased the pain, but would scarcely have converted failure into success. In 1956, when it was Eden's turn to err, the resentment and suspicions of 1954 may have been remembered, but they did not cause miscarriage at Suez, merely made it harder to bear.

12 Epilogue

'It is a well known principle that princes and states are not bound to observe a treaty contrary to their interest.'— CARDINAL ALBERONI[1]

On 23 January 1973 another diplomatic process, which had lasted years rather than months, reached its end: Henry Kissinger, for the United States, and Le Duc Tho, for North Vietnam, initialled an Agreement on Ending the War and Restoring Peace in Vietnam. As the title implies, the purpose was much the same as that of the 1954 Geneva Agreements, but the terms were rather different. The cease-fire was to be 'in place' with no provision for the withdrawal of North Vietnamese forces from the South. No dates had been agreed for a cease-fire in either Cambodia or Laos and the Vietnamese later neither admitted nor implemented the undertaking they were supposed to have given separately to withdraw their forces from these two countries. International supervision of the cease-fire and of restrictions on reinforcement or resupply was entrusted to a balanced commission of Canada, Indonesia, Hungary and Poland fettered by the principle of unanimity. American forces, instead of being ready to withdraw, as the French had been in 1954, when so requested by the government in Saigon, were to be out of the country in two months.

American withdrawal and the release of American prisoners of war did take place. Otherwise, by 30 April 1975, when a helicopter lifted the last US Ambassador out of Saigon just before the city, indeed all of Vietnam, fell to Communist forces, the 1973 Paris Agreement was as dead as if it had never existed. Only in one respect did it resemble its predecessor: it was negotiated behind the back and against the wishes of the government in Saigon.

Why, in 1973, did the United States Government have to settle for terms so much worse than those they rejected in 1954? What had happened in those nineteen and a half years?

136

There are so many possible answers to that question that it needs to be regarded from the narrowly specialised angle of vision proper to this book: the influence of the Geneva Agreements and the rôle of Britain. The Geneva Agreements of 1954 were partially implemented, modified, invoked, given lip service, violated and finally abandoned. They were never forgotten, providing employment for as many propagandists and furnishing matter for as much oratory as the Treaty of Versailles of 1919. Even the Paris Agreement of 1973, which administered the coup de grâce, displayed the cynicism of its drafters by quoting the language and endorsing the principles of Geneva.

Militarily the Geneva Agreements worked reasonably well. Hostilities ceased. In Vietnam the opposing forces did regroup on either side of the demarcation line; the Vietminh left Cambodia; the Pathet Lao withdrew to their northern provinces. When so requested, French forces returned to France. Numerous minor violations by more parties than one were investigated by the International Commissions and featured in their reports.

These reports illustrated one of the more remarkable modifications of the Geneva Agreements. Article 13 of the Final Declaration – an integral component of the Agreements, even if the United States declined to take note of it – provided for members of the Conference 'to consult one another on any question which may be referred to them by the International Supervisory Commission', but did not say how this should be done.[2] A procedure was accordingly invented by the South East Asia Department of the Foreign Office and, once approved in London, agreed with the Soviet Government. It was based on that casual afterthought of 21 July 1954 when Eden and Molotov, as explained in Chapter 10, undertook to devise and circulate proposals for meeting the costs of the three International Supervisory Commissions in Indochina.

It was not until 1956, incidentally, that the proposals put forward by the two governments received the final approval of others concerned and the financial arrangements thus instituted had to be applied, with much dunning, for more years than anyone had at first expected. But the diplomatic process begun by the British Government in the autumn of 1954 early accustomed other governments to the idea that the British and Soviet Foreign Ministers, having assumed at Geneva additional responsibilities as Co-Chairmen of the Conference, should continue in this coordinating rôle even though the Conference was no longer in session.

So reports from the International Commissions were forwarded by the Government of India, which had provided the chairmen of the three commissions, to the British and Soviet Foreign Ministers in their notionally continuing capacity as Co-Chairmen. The Co-Chairmen then circulated the reports, occasionally with agreed comments or proposals of their own, to other governments. This procedure, culminating, in the case of the British Government, in publication of the Commission's report, offered a means of complying with the provisions of Article 13 that was easier and, to most governments concerned, usually more acceptable than any attempt to reconvene the Geneva Conference. Naturally it was not long before others followed the Indian example and addressed to the Co-Chairmen their complaints about the implementation of the Geneva Agreements.

The Co-Chairmen did not always agree, nor did their mediatory influence or the process of consultation they organised often result in any obvious improvement in the observance of the Agreements. It would nevertheless be unduly cynical to describe the only consequence as being a higher standard of hypocrisy. This remarkable international ritual gave those governments which wished to avoid any renewal of hostilities an extra argument for resisting the importunity of allies, clients or sections of public opinion with different priorities. Successive British governments, for instance, found their special position as one of the Co-Chairmen an extremely convenient excuse whenever they had to resist – as, for more than a decade, they were repeatedly required to – conflicting pressures either to quarrel with the United States Government or to give them military assistance. The Soviet Government, whether or not from similar considerations, must also have found the ritual advantageous, or they would not have persisted in it for so long.

There was, after all, no foundation for it in the Geneva Agreements, which do not mention the existence of the Co-Chairmen. The tacit consent given by the Conference to Eden's purely financial proposal of 21 July 1954 could not be construed as authorising transactions far more wide-ranging and long-lasting than anything then envisaged. These were not even preceded by any bilateral agreement between the British and Soviet governments concerning the principles of their cooperation. The concept of Co-Chairmanship evolved, step by step, from a succession of diplomatic exchanges, each related to a particular document, or a specific proposal. The 'Apostolic Succession', however, was established in 1955, when Molotov agreed that Eden, on becoming Prime Minister, should transmit to Macmillan, his successor as Foreign Secretary, the mantle of chairmanship. The precedent was duly followed by the Russians when Molotov was exiled to Outer Mongolia and, although the advent of Gromyko soon made further change superfluous in Moscow, successive British Foreign Secretaries assumed the rôle as part of their office, almost as if it carried the style and title of Defender of the Faith.[3]

Faith in the applicability of the Geneva Agreements was from the outset challenged by the attitude of the United States. After the failure of their persistent efforts to keep the French fighting until American training could produce Vietnamese soldiers to replace them, the United States had reluctantly accepted the cessation of hostilities and the partition of Vietnam. But this sacrifice of half a country to Communism only strengthened American resolve to keep the rest of Indochina in the Free World. Their chosen method was to train and equip the armies of Cambodia, Laos and South Vietnam and to provide all three countries with the backing of the South East Asia Treaty Organisation (SEATO). This American policy was obviously incompatible with the very essence of the Geneva Agreements – which the United States had not, of course, accepted: the reunification of Vietnam through internationally supervised elections and the neutralisation of Cambodia and Laos.

As for SEATO, this zoo of paper tigers had been created by the Manila Treaty of 8 September 1954. It was the price paid by the British for American acquiescence at Geneva in July. SEATO provided a fig-leaf for the nakedness of American policy that was occasionally useful in Washington. But its existence did not deter enemies, nor reassure clients, nor even greatly influence the decisions of its own members. The understandings that mattered were bilateral. SEATO never brought a man or a gun to Indochina and the Alliance had withered and died before the war was over.

The American approach was welcomed in Saigon, where the Geneva Agreements had always been repudiated by the government of Ngo Dinh Diem. An American training mission was established in February 1955 and in October, when Diem should already have been discussing with Hanoi the nation-wide elections envisaged in the Final Declaration, he organised a referendum of his own in the South to sanction his displacement of Bao Dai and proclaimed an independent Republic of Vietnam with himself as President. The North Vietnamese, as the Vietminh must now be called, were unable to react forcibly to this violation of the Geneva Settlement, being preoccupied by the establishment of their authority north of the Demarcation Line, denied military assistance by their allies and, at that time, without an effective revolutionary organisation in the South. They could only protest.

The Co-Chairmanship machine went into high gear, but it was obvious that China and the Soviet Union did not want a resumption of hostilities and Britain was not prepared to quarrel with the United States for any lesser cause than the avoidance of general war. Besides, the United States had a plausible argument: no conceivable level of international supervision would ensure a free election in the North, where Communist pressure on a larger population would be enough to produce an automatic majority even without the minority Communist vote to be expected from the less disciplined South. So the British Co-Chairman did not endorse the proposal of his Soviet colleague for the reconvening of the Geneva Conference. Instead a remarkably anodyne joint message was despatched deploring breaches, urging compliance and exhorting all concerned to keep the peace. That was on 8 May 1956 and, although propaganda and diplomatic activity aimed at implementation of the Geneva Agreements or reconvening the Conference would continue for many years, the prospect of this happening was effectively closed by such an indication that neither the allies nor the principal adversaries of the United States were disposed to apply serious pressure to that end.

Because the consequences, for the United States and still more for the unfortunate peoples of Indochina, of rejecting the Geneva Agreements ultimately proved so much worse than any likely result of their acceptance, there has been a retrospective tendency to blame the British Government for their failure, between July 1954 and July 1956, to remonstrate more vigorously, above all more openly, with the Government of the United States. There was some sympathy, at the time, for this point of view in the South

East Asia Department of the Foreign Office, but it neglected the force of the arguments to the contrary.

Indochina was always of minor concern to the British Government. Only the fear of general war and, a dozen years later, political agitation among the supporters of a Labour Government gave it any standing among important British preoccupations. Most of these demanded American goodwill, if not positive assistance, and the retention of this goodwill had been since 1945, with few exceptions or interruptions, the first objective of British foreign policy. The strain imposed on Anglo-American relations by the events of 1954 had been as unwelcome to the British Government as it had been to their supporters. Moreover, the chances of diverting the United States Government, already emotionally aggrieved and excited, from their chosen policy by further British representations, public or private, were slender. Finally, the basic British contention (not universally shared even in London) that South Vietnam was a rotten apple to be discarded (after what was twenty years later called 'a decent interval') to preserve the neutral integrity of Cambodia and Laos seemed in danger of erosion by events.

In Laos, as a majority of the International Commission agreed in January 1956, the Pathet Lao were obstructing implementation of the political settlement envisaged at Geneva and the chances of compromise were not assisted by the influence of the US Ambassador in Vientiane. A genuinely neutralist Laotian government of national unity would probably not have found acceptance in Hanoi, but the Americans moved in to block it before either the Chinese or the Russians. Cambodia had accepted an United States military mission in 1955 and it was not yet obvious that Prince Sihanouk, who abdicated the throne to become Prime Minister in 1955, would succeed, as he actually did for so many years, in maintaining his country's independence and neutrality. Above all, Ngo Dinh Diem was making quite unexpected progress in establishing his own authority in South Vietnam.

So the British Government acquiesced in American policy in Indochina. So did their successors, sometimes with sympathy, even with all assistance short of help, sometimes with an unconcealed disapproval only moderated by their indigence. After the Communist insurrection in the South had begun in 1959 and as it grew and was nourished by intervention from the North, so the extent first of American advice and assistance, then of actual American participation, expanded. So, unfortunately, did the number of men the government in Hanoi were able and willing to commit to the conflict. As the fighting became ever more violent and spread first to Laos, then to Cambodia, repeated efforts were made, and still more often suggested, whether by the British or by other governments, to promote a diplomatic solution. With the exception of the Geneva Conference of 1961–2, which reached an agreement on Laos neither side made much attempt to honour, these efforts came to nothing. The North Vietnamese, understandably convinced they had been cheated at Geneva in 1954, were no longer interested in anything but the military victory towards which their allies were now willing, at least covertly, to assist them. And, until the people of the United States revolted against the war, American prestige was no less committed to an equal and opposite solution.

On 24 September 1954 Allen Dulles (brother of John Foster and Head of the Central Intelligence Agency) had urged the National Security Council in Washington to give firm support to one leader in South Vietnam. Wilson, the Secretary of Defense, said 'an even more desirable course of action was for the United States to get completely out of the area'.[4] But the Dulles brothers prevailed and, on 23 October 1954, Eisenhower offered Ngo Dinh Diem, the leader of the moment, 'an intelligent programme of American aid ... to assist the government of Vietnam in developing and maintaining a strong viable state, capable of resisting attempted subversion or aggression through military means'.[5] That remained the purpose of the United States until their efforts reached a bitter end on 30 April 1975.

It is a matter of record that the American decision first to support, then to organise and lead, resistance to the Geneva Settlement ushered in many years of atrocious suffering and ended in disaster. It would be the merest flight of fancy to assert that the Geneva Agreements could have been substantially applied in 1956 or soon afterwards; to imagine how this might have been done; or to measure the likely consequences. This is no less true of the opposite hypothesis that occasionally attracts the fantasy of the extreme Right: Britain and France, perhaps others as well, joining the United States in 1954 for wholehearted war on Communism in Asia. The arguments of alternative history are valid only in another world than this. The most that can be said is that it is easier to imagine how the horror of what actually happened could have been mitigated by an opposite American decision in 1954 than it is to suppose that British and French support would have sufficed to turn American failure into success.

Whether or not, as most people thought at the time, there really was a danger of general war in 1954, Eden was justified in describing, on 22 July 1954, the Geneva Agreements as 'a real gain for peace'.[6] They kept not only Britain, but Europe, out of twenty years of futile conflict. There was, however, an unfortunate side-effect. Although the Geneva Settlement was of more enduring advantage to Britain than the other diplomatic achievements of Eden's *annus mirabilis* in 1954 – agreements on Egypt, German rearmament, Iran and Trieste – it also engendered more lasting delusions of grandeur. In 1954 Britain had indeed outfaced the United States and negotiated on equal terms with China and the Soviet Union the peaceful resolution of a major international dispute on a basis first conceived in London. This was nevertheless as much the result of a fortuitous combination of circumstances as of greater foresight or superior diplomatic skill. It was not founded on any balance of real power.

The successes of 1954 may perhaps have exercised a doubly unfortunate influence on Eden in 1956. They probably gave him an exaggerated notion of his ability – and his country's – to manipulate world events. And – because they were genuinely diplomatic successes, achieved by conciliation, compromise, even concession – they were not accepted as such by those diehard Conservatives to whose opinions Eden was particularly sensitive.[7] He was thus predisposed to attempt too much and to prefer a coercive approach.

The after-effects of Geneva bemused the British far beyond 1956. The charade of co-chairmanship, for instance, reached new heights with the 'Wilson initiatives' of the late sixties to promote negotiations on Vietnam and ended by irritating both the Super-Powers.

These later illusions do not detract from the value of the British effort that culminated in the achievement of the 1954 Geneva Agreements on Indochina. The United States were dissuaded from provoking the wider conflict their own leaders professed themselves ready to risk. The French, unable to contrive the means of escape from a predicament they detested, were given time to find a chief capable of decision. The peoples of Indochina were allowed a respite from war and offered the chance, even if it was later snatched away, of a nearer approximation to peace than anything subsequently available. The alternative envisaged in 1954 – victory – did not, as the United States spent 20 years and 45 000 American lives in proving, exist. British hints to this effect were not believed in Washington, but French experience suggests that such advice would have been ignored even if London had borrowed the strident, and much resented, clarity of General de Gaulle. The immolation of Indochina was an American passion Europeans could not prevent, but they may have owed to British efforts the exemption of their own continent. That was 'a real gain for peace'.

Appendix 1: The Seven Points

Characteristics required of an armistice agreement on Indochina for this to be acceptable to the British and United States Governments, as agreed between Eden and Dulles on 29 June 1954.

(FO 371 112075)

(1) Preserves the integrity and independence of Laos and Cambodia and assures the withdrawal of Vietminh forces therefrom.

(2) Preserves at least the southern half of Vietnam, and if possible an enclave in the delta; in this connection we would be unwilling to see the line of division of responsibility drawn further south than a line running generally west from Dong Hoi.

(3) Does not impose on Laos, Cambodia, or retained Vietnam any restrictions materially impairing their capacity to maintain stable non-communist regimes; and especially restrictions impairing their right to maintain adequate forces for internal security, to import arms and to employ foreign advisers.

(4) Does not contain political provisions which would risk loss of the retained area to communist control.

(5) Does not exclude the possibility of the ultimate reunification of Vietnam by peaceful means.

(6) Provides for the peaceful and humane transfer, under international supervision, of those people desiring to be moved from one zone to another of Vietnam; and

(7) Provides effective machinery for international supervision of the agreement.

Appendix 2: The Final Declaration

(*Documents relating to British Involvement in the Indochina Conflict 1945–1965*, Cmnd 2834 Document no. 33 (HMSO, 1965)).

Final Declaration, dated the 21st July, 1954, of the Geneva Conference on the problem of restoring peace in Indochina, in which the representatives of Cambodia, the Democratic Republic of Vietnam, France, Laos, the People's Republic of China, the State of Vietnam, the Union of Soviet Socialist Republics, the United Kingdom and the United States of America took part.

(1) The Conference takes note of the agreements ending hostilities in Cambodia, Laos and Vietnam and organising international control and the supervision of the execution of the provisions of these agreements.

(2) The Conference expresses satisfaction at the ending of hostilities in Cambodia, Laos and Vietnam; the Conference expresses its conviction that the execution of the provisions set out in the present declaration and in the agreements on the cessation of hostilities will permit Cambodia, Laos and Vietnam henceforth to play their part, in full independence and sovereignty, in the peaceful community of nations.

(3) The Conference takes note of the declarations made by the Governments of Cambodia and of Laos of their intention to adopt measures permitting all citizens to take their place in the national community, in particular by participating in the next general elections, which, in conformity with the constitution of each of these countries, shall take place in the course of the year 1955, by secret ballot and in conditions of respect for fundamental freedoms.

(4) The Conference takes note of the clauses in the agreement on the cessation of hostilities in Vietnam prohibiting the introduction into Vietnam of foreign troops and military personnel as well as of all kinds of arms and munitions. The Conference also takes note of the declarations made by the Governments of Cambodia and Laos of their resolution not to request foreign aid, whether in war material, in personnel or in instructors except for the purpose of the effective defence of their territory and, in the case of Laos, to the extent defined by the agreements on the cessation of hostilities in Laos.

(5) The Conference takes note of the clauses in the agreement on the cessation of hostilities in Vietnam to the effect that no military base under the control of a foreign State may be established in the regrouping zones of the two parties, the latter having the obligation to see that the zones allotted to them shall not constitute part of any military alliance and shall not be

146

utilised for the resumption of hostilities or in the service of an aggressive policy. The Conference also takes note of the declarations of the Governments of Cambodia and Laos to the effect that they will not join in any agreement with other States if this agreement includes the obligation to participate in a military alliance not in conformity with the principles of the Charter of the United Nations or, in the case of Laos, with the principles of the agreement on the cessation of hostilities in Laos or, so long as their security is not threatened, the obligation to establish bases on Cambodian or Laotian territory for the military forces of foreign Powers.

(6) The Conference recognises that the essential purpose of the agreement relating to Vietnam is to settle military questions with a view to ending hostilities and that the military demarcation line is provisional and should not in any way be interpreted as constituting a political or territorial boundary. The Conference expresses its conviction that the execution of the provisions set out in the present declaration and in the agreement on the cessation of hostilities creates the necessary basis for the achievement in the near future of a political settlement in Vietnam.

(7) The Conference declares that, so far as Vietnam is concerned, the settlement of political problems, effected on the basis of respect for the principles of independence, unity and territorial integrity, shall permit the Vietnamese people to enjoy the fundamental freedoms, guaranteed by democratic institutions established as a result of free general elections by secret ballot. In order to ensure that sufficient progress in the restoration of peace has been made, and that all the necessary conditions obtain for free expression of the national will, general elections shall be held in July, 1956, under the supervision of an international commission composed of representatives of the member States of the International Supervisory Commission, referred to in the agreement on the cessation of hostilities. Consultations will be held on this subject between the competent representative authorities of the two zones from 20 July, 1955, onwards.

(8) The provisions of the agreements on the cessation of hostilities intended to ensure the protection of individuals and property must be most strictly applied and must, in particular, allow everyone in Vietnam to decide freely in which zone he wishes to live.

(9) The competent representative authorities of the Northern and Southern zones of Vietnam, as well as the authorities of Laos and Cambodia, must not permit any individual or collective reprisals against persons who have collaborated in any way with one of the parties during the war, or against members of such persons' families.

(10) The Conference takes note of the declaration of the Government of the French Republic that it is ready to withdraw its troops from the territory of Cambodia, Laos and Vietnam, at the request of the Governments concerned and within periods which shall be fixed by agreement between the parties except in the cases where, by agreement between the two parties, a certain number of French troops shall remain at specified points and for a specified time.

(11) The Conference takes note of the declaration of the French Government to the effect that for the settlement of all the problems connected with the re-establishment and consolidation of peace in Cambodia, Laos and

Vietnam, the French Government will proceed from the principle of respect for the independence and sovereignty, unity and territorial integrity of Cambodia, Laos and Vietnam.

(12) In their relations with Cambodia, Laos and Vietnam, each member of the Geneva Conference undertakes to respect the sovereignty, the independence, the unity and the territorial integrity of the above-mentioned States, and to refrain from any interference in their internal affairs.

(13) The members of the Conference agree to consult one another on any question which may be referred to them by the International Supervisory Commission, in order to study such measures as may prove necessary to ensure that the agreements on the cessation of hostilities in Cambodia, Laos and Vietnam are respected.

Notes and References

Otherwise unidentified references are to the files in which British public documents are classified in the Public Record Office at Kew.

INTRODUCTION

1. Lord Moran, *Winston Churchill: The Struggle for Survival* (Constable, 1966) p. 405.
2. It should not be supposed that all the British documents are now available. The Joint Intelligence Committee, for instance, usually assessed the situation in Indochina in its weekly summaries and, on several occasions, was asked to produce a special report to assist the process of reaching decisions on British policy. The papers of this Committee constitute only one of several collections not to be found in the Public Record Office. Even those records – of the Cabinet or the Foreign Office, for instance – now open for inspection include many notes that some otherwise unidentified item is still withheld from public gaze. The Foreign Office records, in particular, were more drastically 'weeded' before they reached the Public Record Office than had been the case in earlier years.
3. B. R. Pearn, *An Introduction to the History of South East Asia* (Longmans of Malaya, 1963) p. 5.
4. W. Somerset Maugham, The Door of Opportunity, *Complete Short Stories Vol III* (William Heinemann Ltd, 1951).
5. British Embassy in Paris FO 371 107437.
6. Charles Fenn, *Ho Chi Minh* (Studio Vista, 1973) *passim*.
7. Graham Greene, *The Quiet American* (William Heinemann, 1955).
8. 'Today everyone recognises that it has become imperative to lighten the burden imposed on us by the continuing war in Indochina.' Pierre Mendès France quoted in André Siegfried (ed.), *L'Année Politique 1953* (Presses Universitaires de France, Paris, 1954) p. 47.
9. Of course, the Vietnamese on the French side were suffering more severely, the 1952 casualty ratio being 8 Vietnamese killed: 4 Foreign Legion and North African: 2 French. (Edgar O'Ballance, *The Indochina War 1945–54* (Faber & Faber, 1964) p. 197.) But their puppet government was not a principal in the conflict.
10. A. A. Gromyko and B. N. Ponomarev (eds), *Soviet Foreign Policy Vol II 1945–1980*, 4th ed. (Progress Publishers, Moscow, 1981) p. 198.
11. CAB 129 61.
12. CAB 131 13.

1 FRENCH ATTITUDES AND BRITISH EXPECTATIONS

1. Chancery letter of 24 June 1953, FO 371 107437.
2. 'Three fundamental questions, each involving the national interest . . . economic policy . . . Europe . . . Indochina, that ball and chain we drag with growing impatience.' André Siegfried (ed.), *L'Année Politique 1953* (Presses Universitaires de la France, 1954) p. x.
3. 'France is not on her death bed.' Ibid, p. 55.
4. FO 371 107437.
5. Despatch of 3 July from HM Ambassador Paris, FO 371 107437.
6. FO 371 107437.
7. FO 371 107437.
8. FO 371 106753.
9. FO 371 106768.
10. Foreign Office, *Documents relating to British Involvement in The Indochina Conflict 1945–1965* Cmnd 2834 (HMSO, 1965) p. 11.
11. FO 371 106753.
12. CAB 131 13.
13. CAB 128 26.
14. FO 371 106768.
15. Lord Moran, *Winston Churchill: The Struggle for Survival 1940–1965* (Constable & Co, 1966) p. 411.
16. FO 371 106768.
17. Ibid.
18. On 15 July, FO 371 106754.
19. FO 371 106768.
20. FO 371 106777 and 106778.
21. For full text of Navarre Plan, which was *not* known to the British at the time, see Vincent Auriol, *Journal du Septennat 1947–1954 Vol VII* (Librairie Armand Colin, Paris, 1971) pp. 633–49.
22. 'Victory is certain'. FO 371 106755.
23. FO 371 106754.
24. On 5 August 1953, FO 371 106755.
25. On 15 August 1953, FO 371 106778.
26. FO 371 106743.
27. FO 371 106769.
28. FO 371 106770.
29. FO 371 106769.
30. Hansard Col 213–474.
31. 25 July 1953.
32. FO 371 106777.
33. *The Times*, 16 September 1953.
34. 'To make every effort to break up and destroy the regular forces of the enemy in Indochina.' Siegfried 1953 op. cit. p. 581.
35. On 2 October 1953, FO 371 106770.
36. Siegfried 1953 op. cit. p. 281.

2 WAITING UPON EVENTS

1. FO 371 106779.
2. *Foreign Relations of the United States 1952–54 Volume XIII Part 1: Indochina*, ed. Neal H. Petersen (US Govt. Printing Office, Washington, 1982) pp. 762-6.
3. DEFE 4 65.
4. DEFE 4 66.
5. FO 371 106768.
6. FO 371 106771.
7. 2 October 1953 FO 371 106770.
8. 'The additional American aid is not intended to keep the war in Indochina going, but to finish it.' André Siegfried (ed.) *L'Année Politique 1953* (Presses Universitaires de France, Paris, 1954) p. 276.
9. FO 371 106756.
10. *L'Année Politique 1953* op. cit. p. 291.
11. FO 371 106771.
12. 28 October 1953 FO 371 106757.
13. FO 371 106779.
14. Vincent Auriol, *Journal du Septennat Vol VII 1953–54* (Librairie Armand Colin, Paris, 1971) pp. 301 and 779.
15. Ibid pp. 818–19.
16. General Navarre's own account (Henri Navarre, *Agonie de l'Indochine (1953–54)*, (Paris, Librairie Plon 1956.)) has been amplified and qualified by other writers but not contradicted. He says the principle of reinforcements was agreed on 24 July 1953, but not their extent. In August he had to put forward reduced demands, but these were rejected on 11 September, a decision against which he protested at the beginning of October. On 4 December he was informed of the decision reached by the Committee of National Defence on 13 November to send no further reinforcements. He says (pp. 104 and 106) that only on 10 April 1954 did the French Government decide to send him reinforcements, but on p. 105 that he had been sent 8 battalions of infantry, an artillery group and an engineer battalion. But neither he nor anyone else says whether these units arrived in 1953 or 1954.
17. General Delmas of the Service Historique de l'Armée de Terre at Vincennes was kind enough to supply the author with copies of reports compiled by the French General Staff in Saigon on 24 July 1953 and 22 January 1954. These give the strength 'des effectifs des forces régulières françaises terrestres, aeriennes et navales en Extrême-Orient' (of the operational personnel of regular French land, air and naval forces in the Far East) on 1 July 1953 and 1 January 1954 respectively. The figures are broken down by service, national origin and sex, but do not indicate units or formations. Although a true comparison would require analysis of the order of battle, the information they give is nevertheless both new and authentic.
18. FO 371 106779.
19. Ibid.
20. David Carlton, *Anthony Eden* (Allen Lane, 1981) p. 330.

21. Lord Moran, *Winston Churchill: The Struggle for Survival 1940–1965* (Constable, 1966) p. 418.
22. Anthony Nutting – essay on Sir Anthony Eden in Herbert van Thal, *The Prime Ministers* (George Allen & Unwin, 1975) p. 334. Sir Anthony Nutting confirmed this view in an interview with the author on 18 October 1984, adding that he believed vanity, including in that term an excessive confidence in his own capacity, to have been the dominant influence on Eden's decisions.
23. Quoted by permission of Sir Evelyn Shuckburgh from the unpublished diary of which he kindly allowed the author to read the volumes for 1953 and 1954.
24. *The Times*, 9 October 1953.
25. FO 371 106770.
26. CAB 129 64.
27. François Joyaux, *La Chine et le règlement du premier conflit d'Indochine (Genève, 1954)* (Publications de la Sorbonne, Paris, 1979) p. 39. The author had access to unpublished reports in the archives of the French Foreign Ministry.
28. Townsend Hoopes, *The Devil and John Foster Dulles* (André Deutsch, 1974) p. 491.
29. Ibid p. 158.
30. Joyaux op. cit. p. 93.
31. FO 371 106771.
32. FO 371 103710.
33. FO 371 106749, for full text see Document 12 in Foreign Office, *Documents relating to British Involvement in the Indochina Conflict 1945–1965*, Cmnd 2834 (HMSO, 1965).
34. 16 December 1953 FO 371 106749.
35. 'An honourable solution . . . a diplomatic solution of the conflict'. Jean Lacouture and Philippe Devillers, *La Fin d'Une Guerre: Indochine 1954* (Editions du Seuil, Paris, 1960) pp. 43–4 and *L'Année Politique 1953* op. cit. p. 303.
36. *Foreign Relations of the United States* op. cit. pp. 887–8.
37. The importance of these lapses from the formal politeness expected by foreigners is illustrated by their citation, a quarter of a century later, in a brief reference to the Bermuda Conference by a serious French historian, Paul Marie de la Gorce, *Apogée et Mort de la IVe République* (Bernard Grasset, Paris, 1979) p. 110.
38. 2 December 1953 FO 371 106749.
39. Moran op. cit. pp. 503–12.
40. Sir Evelyn Shuckburgh, diary.
41. Information from Sir Evelyn Shuckburgh and Moran op. cit.
42. 3 December 1953 FO 371 107434.
43. *Foreign Relations of the United States* op. cit. pp. 758–9.
44. Ibid, p. 923.
45. Ibid, p. 897.
46. Ibid, *Vol V: International Conferences* pp. 1825 and 1828.
47. FO 371 106771.
48. *Foreign Relations of the United States, Vol XIII Part 1* pp. 901–2.
49. 9 December 1953 FO 371 106771 and 16 December FO 371 106779.

50. FO 371 106771.
51. 17 December 1953 FO 371 107434 and *L'Année Politique 1953* op. cit. p. 447.
52. 14 and 15 December 1953. Sir Anthony Eden, *Full Circle* (Cassell, 1960) p. 57.
53. 'As the end of M. Auriol's term draws near, the meetings of the Government become less frequent.' *L'Année Politique 1953* op. cit. pp. 83–9.
54. *Foreign Relations of the United States Vol XIII Part 1* pp. 929–31.
55. FO 371 106757.
56. FO 371 106779.
57. 29 December 1953 FO 371 106757.
58. FO 371 106779.

3   CHANGING COURSE

1. FO 371 112049.
2. FO 371 112047.
3. *Foreign Relations of the United States 1952–54 Vol XIII: Indochina*, ed. Neal H. Petersen (US Govt Printing Office, Washington, 1982) Part 1, pp. 937–8.
4. Ibid p. 942.
5. Ibid pp. 947–54.
6. *The Times* 14 January 1954.
7. See in Chapter 2.
8. On 18 January 1954 FO 371 112024.
9. Diary of Sir Evelyn Shuckburgh.
10. CAB 128 27.
11. Foreign Office, *Documents Relating to the Meeting of Foreign Ministers of France, the United Kingdom, the Soviet Union and the United States of America: Berlin, January 25–February 18 1954*, Cmnd 9080 (HMSO, 1954).
12. Georges Bidault, *D'Une Résistance à l'Autre* (Les Presses du Siècle 1965) p. 193.
13. Told to the author in 1984 by Sir Andrew Stark (in 1954 Assistant Private Secretary to Eden).
14. Diary of Sir Evelyn Shuckburgh. The memorandum in which Eden explained to the Cabinet his objectives in the Conference dismissed the idea of a five-power Meeting as 'not suitable for discussion at Berlin'. (Circulated on 11 January 1954, CAB 129 65.)
15. To the Cabinet on 22 February 1954 CAB 128 27.
16. *Foreign Relations of the United States* op. cit. *Vol XVI* p. 416.
17. Foreign Office, Cmnd 9080, op. cit.
18. François Joyaux, *La Chine et le Règlement du Premier Conflit d'Indochine: Genève 1954* (Publications de la Sorbonne, Paris, 1979) p. 104.
19. President Dwight D. Eisenhower, *Mandate for Change 1953–1956* (Heinemann, 1963) p. 343.
20. FO 371 112047.
21. Chapter 2 p. 39.
22. FO 371 112048 (version of 17 March) and FO 271 112049 (version of 31 March).

23. My diary records Denis Allen and John Tahourdin as surprised and gratified by the vigour of the support received from the Chiefs of Staff, whose views had been awaited with some apprehension.

24. Jean Lacouture and Philippe Devillers, *La Fin d'une Guerre: Indochine 1954* (Editions du Seuil Paris, 1960) pp. 62–5.

25. *Foreign Relations of the United States* op. cit. *Vol XIII Part I* pp. 1030–1.

26. Ibid, pp. 1063–4.

27. Ibid, p. 945.

28. Ibid, pp. 947–54.

29. Ibid, pp. 971–6.

30. CAB 129 67.

31. FO 371 112047.

32. Ibid.

33. On 31 January 1954, Ibid.

34. *Foreign Relations of the United States* op. cit. *Vol XIII Part I* p. 1096.

35. 'We are in fact now unanimous in wishing to settle the conflict by way of negotiations.' André Siegfried (ed.), *L'Année Politique 1954* (Presses Universitaires de France, Paris, 1955) p. 12.

36. Lacouture, op. cit. p. 65.

37. *Foreign Relations of the United States* op. cit. *Vol XIII Part I* pp. 1137–40 and FO 371 112048.

38. Lacouture op. cit. p. 73.

39. Ibid, p. 74 and Paul Ely, *L'Indochine dans la Tourmente* (Plon, Paris, 1964) pp. 82, 84–5.

40. FO 371 112048.

41. FO 371 112049.

42. *Foreign Relations of the United States* op. cit. *Vol XIII Part I* p. 1187.

43. Mr. Emrys Hughes on 15 March 1954. Hansard Vol 525 Col 11.

44. FO 371 112049.

45. *Foreign Relations of the United States* op. cit. Vol XIII Part I p. 1203.

4 THE CRISIS OF APRIL

1. Report to National Security Council. *Foreign Relations of the United States 1952–54 Vol XIII: Indonesia* ed. Neal H. Petersen (US Govt Printing Office, Washington, 1982) *Part I* pp. 1250–65.

2. From a description written by Sir Denis Allen in 1970 and kindly communicated to the author.

3. Written on 30 June 1954 by the then Australian Minister for External Affairs. T. B. Millar (ed.), *Australian Foreign Minister: The Diaries of R. G. Casey 1951–60* (Collins, 1972).

4. See note 2.

5. Interview given to *Life* magazine in January 1956. Quoted in Townsend Hoopes *The Devil and John Foster Dulles* (André Deutsch, 1974).

6. On 1 May 1954 *Foreign Relations of the United States*, op. cit. *Vol XVI* pp. 648–9.

7. FO 371 112058.

8. Robert F. Randle, *Geneva 1954: The Settlement of the Indochina War* (Princeton University Press, 1969) p. 71.
9. FO 371 112053.
10. *Pentagon Papers (Senator Gravel Edition) Vol I* (Beacon Press, Boston, 1971).
11. *Foreign Relations of the United States*, op. cit. *Vol XIII* pp. 1220–23.
12. Ibid pp. 1163–8.
13. Admiral Arthur W. Radford, *From Pearl Harbor to Vietnam*, ed. Stephen Josika Jr. (Hoover Institution Press, Stanford University, Stanford, California, 1980) pp. 394–5.
14. *Foreign Relations of the United States*, op. cit. *Vol XIII* pp. 1201–2.
15. Victor Bator, *Vietnam: A Diplomatic Tragedy: Origins of US Involvement* (Faber & Faber, 1967) p. 57.
16. *Foreign Relations of the United States*, op. cit. *Vol XIII* pp. 1236–8.
17. Ibid, pp. 1241–2.
18. Radford, op. cit. p. 420.
19. CAB 129 68 (a retrospective account).
20. FO 371 112049.
21. On 4 April 1954. FO 371 112050.
22. Ibid.
23. FO 371 112051.
24. FO 371 112050.
25. *Foreign Relations of the United States*, op. cit. *Vol XIII* pp. 1250–65.
26. FO 371 112050.
27. CAB 128 27.
28. My diary.
29. FO 371 112051.
30. *Foreign Relations of the United States*, op. cit. *Vol XIII*, pp. 1231–5.
31. My diary.
32. FO 371 112053.
33. FO 371 112054.
34. Ibid.
35. *Foreign Relations of the United States*, op. cit. *Vol XIII* pp. 1307–9.
36. CAB 131 101.
37. *Foreign Relations of the United States*, op. cit. *Vol XIII* p. 1322.
38. Hansard Vol 526 Cols 969–75.
39. *Foreign Relations of the United States*, op. cit. *Vol XIII* pp. 1331–4.
40. FO 371 112055. A minute by Churchill in PREM 11 645 confirms that he, too, said nothing of the kind.
41. FO 371 112053.
42. Ibid.
43. Sir Anthony Eden, *Full Circle* (Cassell, 1960) p. 99.
44. FO 371 112053.
45. Hoopes, op. cit. p. 216.
46. FO 371 112053.
47. *Foreign Relations of the United States* op. cit. *Vol XIII* p. 1322.
48. FO 371 112051.
49. FO 371 112048.
50. FO 371 112051.
51. Diary of Sir Evelyn Shuckburgh.

52. *Foreign Relations of the United States*, op. cit. *Vol XIII* pp. 1361–2 and PREM 11 645.
53. FO 371 112055.
54. FO 371 112057.
55. Vincent Auriol, *Journal du Septennat 1947–1954 Vol VII 1953–1954* ed. Jacques Ozouf (Librairie Armand Colin, Paris, 1971) pp. 511–12.
56. FO 371 112055.
57. *Foreign Relations of the United States*, op. cit. *Vol XIII* p. 1397.
58. FO 371 112056.
59. *Foreign Relations of the United States*, op. cit. *Vol XIII* p. 1397.
60. Diary of Sir Evelyn Shuckburgh and CAB 129 68.
61. François Joyaux, *La Chine et le Règlement du Premier Conflit d'Indochine: Genève 1954* (Publications de la Sorbonne, Paris, 1979) p. 82, and Paul Ely *L'Indochine dans la Tourmente* (Plon, Paris, 1964) p. 90.
62. *Foreign Relations of the United States*, op. cit. *Vol XIII* pp. 1270–2.
63. CAB 129 68.
64. Diary of Sir Evelyn Shuckburgh.
65. *Foreign Relations of the United States*, op. cit. *Vol XIII* pp. 1250–65.
66. That issued on 13 April 1954 after the Eden–Dulles meetings. See p. 57.
67. CAB 129 68.
68. FO 371 112058.
69. *Foreign Relations of the United States*, op. cit. *Vol XVI* pp. 553–7.
70. FO 371 112056.
71. *Foreign Relations of the United States*, op. cit. *Vol XVI* pp. 553–7.
72. Diary of Sir Evelyn Shuckburgh.
73. *Foreign Relations of the United States*, op. cit. *Vol XVI* p. 607.
74. FO 371 112056, 112057 and 112059.
75. CAB 128 27.
76. FO 371 112059.

5 GENEVA: TUNING UP

1. Sir Anthony Eden, *Full Circle* (Cassell, 1960) p. 108.
2. François Joyaux, *La Chine et le Règlement du Premier Conflit d'Indochine: Genève 1954* (Publications de la Sorbonne, Paris, 1979) pp. 117–18.
3. Jean Chauvel, *Commentaire Vol III – De Berne à Paris (1952–1962)* (Fayard, Paris, 1973) p. 63.
4. Diary of Sir Evelyn Shuckburgh.
5. T. B. Millar (ed.), *Australian Foreign Minister: The Diaries of R. G. Casey 1951–60* (Collins, 1972) p. 141.
6. FO 371 112057.
7. FO 371 112059.
8. FO 371 112060.
9. 'The Government only survived because it could not manage to fall.' André Siegfried (ed.), *L'Année Politique 1954* (Presses Universitaires de France, Paris, 1955) p. xii.

10. FO 371 112060 and *Foreign Relations of the United States 1952–54 Vol XIII: Indochina*, ed. Neal H. Petersen (US Govt Printing Office, Washington, 1982) Part 2 pp. 1502–3.
11. FO 371 113057.
12. *Foreign Relations of the United States*, op. cit. *Vol XIII Part 2* p. 1467.
13. Diary of Sir Evelyn Shuckburgh.
14. FO 371 112058.
15. Diary of Sir Evelyn Shuckburgh.
16. FO 371 112059.
17. FO 371 112060.
18. FO 371 112064.
19. Eden, op. cit. p. 143.
20. Rather a small, thin man whose face, all bumps and furrows, made him look as if he had chewed some bitter pill. He did in fact have stomach trouble and was thus prone to attacks of indigestion and to brief but violent fits of temper . . . an intelligent man, who appreciated what was concrete, understood politics and did not deal in false coin. Chauvel, op. cit. p. 56.

6 PRELUDE AND FUGUE

1. Foreign Office *Documents relating to the discussion of Korea and Indochina at the Geneva Conference: April 27–June 15 1954*, Cmnd 9186 (HMSO).
2. Diary of Sir Evelyn Shuckburgh, 30 April 1954.
3. Cmnd 9186, op. cit.
4. Diary of Sir Evelyn Shuckburgh, 5 May 1954.
5. Jean Chauvel, *Commentaire Vol III – De Berne à Paris (1952–1962)* (Fayard, Paris, 1973) p. 58.
6. FO 371 112061.
7. FO 371 112062.
8. FO 371 112066.
9. On 5 May 1954. PREM 11 649.
10. Jean Lacouture and Philippe Devillers, *La Fin d'Une Guerre: Indochine 1954* (Editions du Seuil Paris, 1960) p. 149.
11. FO 371 112060.
12. FO 371 112058.
13. Humphrey Trevelyan, *Worlds Apart* (Macmillan, 1971) p. 78.
14. FO 371 112065.
15. Sir Anthony Eden, *Full Circle* (Cassel & Co, 1960). The account on p. 119 does not fully reflect the reports sent by Eden at the time.
16. *Foreign Relations of the United States 1952–54 Vol XIII: Indochina*, ed. Neal H. Petersen (US Govt Printing Office, Washington, 1982) Part 2 pp. 1566–8.
17. FO 371 112065, 112066 and 112067.
18. *The Times*, 19 May 1954.
19. Hansard Vol 527 Cols 1691–4.
20. Hansard Vol 527 Cols 2291–2.
21. *Foreign Relations of the United States*, op. cit. *Vol XVI* pp. 815–6.

22. FO 371 112066.
23. On 10 May 1954. Cmnd 9186, op. cit.
24. FO 371 112067.
25. FO 371 112067.
26. FO 371 112058.
27. FO 371 112071.
28. FO 371 112060.
29. *Foreign Relations of the United States*, op. cit. *Vol XIII* Part 2 pp. 1667–9.
30. Ibid, pp. 1590–2.

7   RESTRICTED SESSIONS: RESTRICTED RESULTS

1. On 20 May 1954. *Foreign Relations of the United States 1952–54 Vol XVI: The Geneva Conference*, ed. Neal H. Petersen (US Govt Printing Office, Washington, 1981) p. 865.
2. FO 371 112067.
3. Ibid.
4. See note 1.
5. FO 371 112067.
6. FO 371 112069.
7. Ministry of Foreign Affairs, Socialist Republic of Vietnam, *The Truth About Vietnam – China Relations Over the Last Thirty Years: 1979* (Printed in Vancouver, Canada, 1980) p. 22.
8. FO 371 112048.
9. For instance, on 3 May 1954, M. Dejean, the French High Commissioner in Saigon. Jean Lacouture and Philippe Devillers, *La Fin d'une Guerre: Indochine 1954* (Editions du Seuil Paris, 1960) p. 123.
10. FO 371 112059.
11. FO 371 112070.
12. See p. 53.
13. FO 371 112065.
14. FO 371 112069.
15. FO 371 112067.
16. Ibid.
17. PREM 11 649.
18. FO 371 112069.
19. FO 371 112067.
20. Ibid. The objection actually emanated from the Associated States FO 371 112068.
21. FO 371 112068.
22. François Joyaux *La Chine et le Règlement du Premier Conflit d'Indochine: Genève 1954* (Publications de la Sorbonne, Paris, 1979) p. 199.
23. Ibid pp. 236–7.
24. *Foreign Relations of the United States*, op. cit. *Vol XVI* p. 1169.
25. PREM 11 649.

26. Information given to the author in 1984 by Sir Andrew Stark, who was at Geneva in 1954 as Eden's Assistant Private Secretary.
27. Joyaux, op. cit. pp. 119–20.
28. Humphrey Trevelyan, *Worlds Apart* (Macmillan 1971) pp. 86–8.
29. FO 371 112068.
30. Sir Anthony Eden, *Full Circle* (Cassell, 1960) p. 127.
31. *Foreign Relations of the United States*, op. cit. *Vol XVI* pp. 974–8.
32. Letter to the author in 1984.
33. *Foreign Relations of the United States*, op. cit. *Vol XVI* pp. 886–7.
34. 'Towards his foreign partners he had the best conference table manners I have ever seen.' Jean Chauvel, *Commentaire Vol III – De Berne à Paris (1952–1962)* (Fayard, Paris, 1973) p. 57.
35. *Foreign Relations of the United States*, op. cit. *Vol XIII Part 2* pp. 1641–4.
36. CAB 128 27 and CAB 129 68.
37. On 26 May 1954. FO 371 112069.
38. Hansard Vol 527 Cols 2291–2.
39. FO 371 112068.
40. FO 371 112060 and PREM 11 649.
41. FO 371 112069.

8 PHOENIX FROM THE ASHES

1. FO 371 112070.
2. *The Times*, 4 June 1954.
3. FO 371 112069.
4. *Foreign Relations of the United States 1952–54 Vol XVI: The Geneva Conference*, ed. Neal H. Petersen (US Govt Printing Office, Washington, 1981) p. 1014.
5. FO 371 112069.
6. CAB 128 27.
7. FO 371 112073.
8. FO 371 112105.
9. FO 371 112068.
10. FO 371 112106.
11. FO 371 112069.
12. FO 371 112072.
13. FO 371 112070. See p. 89.
14. FO 371 112071.
15. Robert F. Randle, *Geneva 1954: The Settlement of the Indochina War* (Princeton University Press, 1969) p. 240.
16. Sir Anthony Eden, *Full Circle* (Cassell, 1960) p. 128.
17. Anthony Seldon, *Churchill's Indian Summer* (Hodder & Stoughton, 1981) p. 47.
18. FO 371 112070 and 112071.
19. FO 371 112073.
20. *Pentagon Papers (Senator Gravel Edition) Vol I* (Beacon Press, Boston, 1971) p. 597.

21. Victor Bator, *Vietnam: A Diplomatic Tragedy: Origins of US Involvement* (Faber & Faber, 1967) p. 92.

22. Jean Lacouture and Philippe Devillers, *La Fin d'une Guerre: Indochine 1954* (Editions du Seuil, 1960) p. 202.

23. François Joyaux, *La Chine et le Règlement du Premier Conflit d'Indochine: Genève 1954* (Publications de la Sorbonne, Paris, 1979) pp. 202–3.

24. FO 371 112070.

25. *Foreign Relations of the United States*, op. cit. *Vol XIII Part 2* pp. 1670–2.

26. Ibid pp. 1667–9.

27. Ibid pp. 1687–9.

28. Ibid p. 1720.

29. Ibid pp. 1713–19.

30. FO 371 112072.

31. FO 371 112073.

32. Ministry of Foreign Affairs, Socialist Republic of Vietnam, *The Truth About Vietnam-China Relations Over The Last Thirty Years 1979* (Printed in Vancouver, Canada, 1980) p. 5.

33. Ibid, p. 20.

34. Hoang van Hoan, 'Distortion of Facts About Militant Friendship Between Viet Nam and China is Impermissible' *Beijing Review*, no. 49, 7 December 1979.

35. 'No historical work has ever been produced in the People's Republic of China which deals, directly or indirectly, with the attitude of the government in Peking to the question of Indochina in 1954.' Joyaux op. cit. p. 13.

36. FO 371 112073.

37. FO 371 112074.

38. Diary of Sir Evelyn Shuckburgh.

39. CAB 128 27.

40. *Foreign Relations of the United States*, op. cit. *Vol XVI* p. 1189.

41. FO 371 112074.

42. CAB 129 69.

9   FRANCE TAKES THE LEAD

1. 'Since we resumed office' (the report was intended for Churchill) meant since October 1951. FO 371 112077.

2. See p. 15.

3. Joseph Laniel, *Jours de Gloire et Jours Cruels 1908–1958* (Presses de la Cité, Paris, 1971) pp. 267–9.

4. 'I shall appear before you by the 20th of July and report the outcome. If no satisfactory solution has been forthcoming by that date . . . my government will submit their resignation to the President of the Republic.' Jean Lacouture, *Pierre Mendès France* (Editions du Seuil, Paris 1981) p. 23.

5. FO 371 112108.

6. See p. 15.

7. FO 371 112075.

8. *Foreign Relations of the United States 1952–54 Vol XIII Part 2*, ed. Neal H. Petersen (US Govt Printing Office, Washington, 1982) pp. 1726–7.
9. Ibid, pp. 1608–9.
10. Ibid, pp. 1782–4.
11. FO 371 112107.
12. FO 371 112074.
13. Sir Anthony Eden, *Full Circle* (Cassell, 1960) p. 130.
14. PREM 11 649.
15. CAB 128 27.
16. Harold Macmillan, *Tides of Fortune* (Macmillan, 1969) p. 532.
17. FO 371 112075.
18. 'The man was impressive.' Pierre Mendès France, *Choisir* (Stock, Paris, 1974) p. 58 and FO 371 112075.
19. FO 371 112075.
20. FO 371 112076.
21. *Foreign Relations of the United States*, op. cit. *Vol XVI* pp. 1267–8 and 1291–2.
22. FO 371 112076 and 112077.
23. FO 371 112108.
24. FO 371 112075.
25. PREM 11 649.
26. *Foreign Relations of the United States*, op. cit. *Vol XIII Part 2* pp. 1620–1.
27. Ibid pp. 1741–3, 1748–51.
28. FO 371 112075.
29. FO 371 112076.
30. FO 371 112075.
31. PREM 11 649.
32. Hansard Vol 529 Cols 428–550.
33. Eden op. cit. p. 133.
34. FO 371 112075.
35. *The Times*, 29 June 1954.
36. FO 371 112075.
37. FO 371 112076.
38. On 12 July. Hansard Vol 530 Col 43.
39. *Foreign Relations of the United States*, op. cit. *Vol XVI* p. 1282.
40. Ibid, *Vol XIII Part 2* p. 1788.
41. FO 371 112076.
42. *Foreign Relations of the United States*, op. cit. *Vol XIII Part 2* p. 1807.
43. FO 371 112077.
44. Hansard Vol 530 Col 491.

10 LAST ACT

1. At a press conference on 21 July 1954, FO 371 112081.
2. FO 371 112068.
3. FO 371 112078.
4. Jean Lacouture, *Pierre Mendès France* (Editions du Seuil, Paris, 1981) p. 248.
5. FO 371 112078.

6. FO 371 112079.
7. FO 371 112085.
8. FO 371 112078.
9. FO 371 112080.
10. FO 371 112079.
11. PREM 11 650.
12. *Foreign Relations of the United States 1952–54 Vol XVI Geneva Conference*, ed. Neal H. Petersen (US Govt Printing Office, Washington, 1981) p. 1430.
13. FO 371 112079 and 112080.
14. François Joyaux, *La Chine et le Règlement du Premier Conflit d'Indochine: Genève 1954* (Publications de la Sorbonne, Paris, 1979) p. 291.
15. CAB 128 27.
16. FO 371 112080.
17. Ministry of Foreign Affairs, Socialist Republic of Vietnam, *The Truth About Vietnam-China Relations Over The Last Thirty Years 1979* (Printed in Vancouver, Canada, 1980) p. 23.
18. Joyaux op. cit. p. 293.
19. *Foreign Relations of the United States*, op. cit. p. 1479.
20. FO 371 112080.
21. Foreign Office, *Further Documents relating to the discussion of Indochina at the Geneva Conference: June 16–July 21 1954* Cmd 9239 (HMSO, 1954), *passim*.
22. Ibid pp. 8–9.
23. Harold Macmillan, *Tides of Fortune* (Macmillan, 1969) p. 536.
24. Hansard Vol 530 Cols 1570–4.
25. Lord Moran, *Winston Churchill: The Struggle for Survival, 1940–1965* (Constable, 1966) p. 581.
26. 'The French task in Indochina', FO 371 112082 and 112083.
27. Joyaux op. cit. pp. 296–7, 301–3.
28. FO 371 112082.
29. PREM 11 650.
30. A. A. Gromyko and B. N. Ponomarev (eds), *Soviet Foreign Policy Vol II 1945–1980* trans. David Skvirsky (Progress Publishers, Moscow 4th ed., 1981) p. 202.
31. FO 371 113084.
32. FO 371 112081 and 112082.
33. FO 371 112084.

11 MYTHS

1. David Carlton, *Anthony Eden* (Allen Lane, 1981) p. 344.
2. *Foreign Relations of the United States 1952–54 Vol XIII: Indochina*, ed. Neal H. Petersen (US Govt Printing Office, Washington, 1982) pp. 718–9.
3. Ibid, pp. 258–9.
4. Ibid, p. 923.
5. André Siegfried, *L'Année Politique 1953* (Presses Universitaires de France, Paris, 1954) p. 424.
6. FO 371 107434.

7. On 23 February 1954. *Foreign Relations of the United States*, op. cit. *Vol V* p. 879.
8. 'Adenauer cannot be exchanged for Ho Chi Minh.' André Siegfried, *L'Année Politique 1954* (Presses Universitaires de France, Paris, 1955) p. 329.
9. *Foreign Relations of the United States*, op. cit. *Vol V* p. 885.
10. Ibid, *Vol XIII* p. 1337.
11. Ibid, *Vol V* pp. 957–9.
12. Joseph Laniel, *Jours de Gloire et Jours Cruels 1908–1958* (Presses de la Cité, Paris, 1971) pp. 267–9.
13. Siegfried, op. cit. 1955 p. 400.
14. 'In so delicate a matter, no solution can be regarded as good, even as admissible, if it has to be imposed by a bare majority on an ardent minority; wide national support is required.' Ibid p. 393.
15. Jean Lacouture, *Pierre Mendès France* (Editions du Seuil Paris, 1981) pp. 246–7.
16. Siegfried op. cit. 1955 p. 400.
17. Lord Gladwyn, *Memoirs* (Weidenfeld & Nicolson, 1972) pp. 271–2.
18. p. 60.
19. Carlton, op. cit. p. 301.
20. T. B. Millar, *Australian Foreign Minister: The Diaries of R. G. Casey 1951–60* (Collins, 1972) p. 163.
21. FO 371 103523.

12 EPILOGUE

1. This dictum by a Spanish Foreign Minister was uttered in 1717. James Cable, *Diplomacy at Sea* (Macmillan, 1985) p. 13.
2. See p. 148.
3. The authoritative account of the evolution of the Co-Chairmanship is that by the late Professor Pearn in the narrative section of *Documents Relating to British Involvement in the Indochina Conflict 1945–1965*, Cmnd 2834 (HMSO, 1965).
4. *Foreign Relations of the United States 1952–54 Vol XIII Part 2: Indochina*, ed. Neal H. Petersen (US Govt Printing Office, Washington, 1982) p. 2059.
5. R. B. Smith, *An International History of the Vietnam War Vol I: Revolution versus Containment 1955–61* (Macmillan, 1983) p. 35.
6. *Hansard* Vol 530 Cols 1570–4.
7. Eden's latest biographer seems to share the diehard view: 'It is therefore ironic that claims that Eden had an *annus mirabilis* should have to rest so largely on so ultimately unheroic a performance as Geneva represented.' Unheroic or merely unwelcome to the United States? David Carlton, *Anthony Eden* (Allen Lane, 1981) p. 356.

Select Bibliography

Auriol, Vincent, *Journal du Septennat 1947–1954 Vol VII – 1953–1954* (ed. Jacques Ozouf) (Librairie Armand Colin, Paris, 1971).

Bator, Victor, *Vietnam: A Diplomatic Tragedy: Origins of US Involvement* (Faber & Faber Ltd, 1967).

Bidault, Georges, *D'Une Résistance à l'Autre* (Les Presses du Siècle, 1965).

Carlton, David, *Anthony Eden* (Allen Lane, 1981).

Chauvel, Jean, *Commentaires Vol III – De Berne à Paris (1952–1962)* (Fayard, Paris, 1973).

Eden, Sir Anthony, *Full Circle* (Cassell & Co. Ltd, 1960).

Eisenhower, President Dwight D., *Mandate for Change 1953–1956* (Heinemann, 1963).

Ely, Paul, *L'Indochine dans la Tourmente* (Plon, Paris, 1964).

Finer, Herman, *Dulles over Suez* (Heinemann, 1964).

Foreign Office, *Documents Relating to the Meeting of Foreign Ministers of France, the United Kingdom, the Soviet Union and the United States of America: Berlin, January 25–February 18 1954*, Cmnd 9080 (HMSO).

Foreign Office, *Documents relating to the discussion of Korea and Indochina at the Geneva Conference April 27–June 15 1954*, Cmnd 9186 (HMSO).

Foreign Office, *Further Documents relating to the discussion of Indochina at the Geneva Conference: June 16–July 21 1954*, Cmnd 9239 (HMSO, 1954).

Foreign Office, *Documents relating to British Involvement in the Indochina Conflict 1945–1965*, Cmnd 2834 (HMSO, 1965).

Foreign Relations of the United States 1952–54 Vol V (Parts 1 and 2): Western European Security, ed. John A. Bernbaum, Lisle A. Rose and Charles S. Sampson, 1983. *Vol XIII (Parts 1 and 2): Indochina*, ed. Neal H. Petersen, 1982; *Vol XVI: The Geneva Conference*, 1981 (US Govt Printing Office, Washington).

Gras, Général Yves, *Histoire de la Guerre d'Indochine* (Librairie Plon, Paris, 1979).

Gromyko, A. A. and Ponomarev, B. N. (eds) *Soviet Foreign Policy Vol II 1945–1980*. Trans. David Skvirksy (Progress Publishers, Moscow 4th ed., 1981).

Hoopes, Townsend, *The Devil and John Foster Dulles* (André Deutsch, 1974).

Joyaux, François, *La Chine et le Règlement du Premier Conflit d'Indochine: Genève 1954* (Publications de la Sorbonne, Paris, 1979).

Kissinger, Henry, *The White House Years* (Weidenfeld & Nicolson and Michael Joseph, 1979).

Kissinger, Henry, *Years of Upheaval* (Weidenfeld & Nicolson and Michael Joseph, 1982).

Lacouture, Jean and Devillers, Philippe, *La Fin d'une Guerre: Indochine 1954* (Editions du Seuil, Paris, 1960).

Lacouture, Jean, *Pierre Mendès France* (Editions du Seuil, Paris, 1981).

Select Bibliography 165

Laniel, Joseph, *Jours de Gloire et Jours Cruels 1908–1958* (Presses de la Cité, Paris, 1971).

Ministry of Foreign Affairs, Socialist Republic of Vietnam, *The Truth About Vietnam-China Relations Over the Last Thirty Years 1979* (printed in Vancouver, Canada, 1980).

Moran, Lord, *Winston Churchill: The Struggle for Survival 1940–1965* (Constable, 1966).

Navarre, Henri, *Agonie de l'Indochine (1953–54)* (Librairie Plon, Paris, 1956).

Radford, Admiral Arthur W., *From Pearl Harbor to Vietnam*, ed. Stephen Jurika Jr (Hoover Institution Press, Stanford University, California, 1980).

Randle, Robert F., *Geneva 1954: The Settlement of the Indochina War* (Princeton Univ. Press, 1969).

Seldon, Anthony, *Churchill's Indian Summer* (Hodder & Stoughton, 1981).

Siegfried, André (ed.), *L'Année Politique 1953* (Presses Universitaires de France, Paris, 1954).

Siegfried, André (ed.), *L'Année Politique 1954* (Presses Universitaires de France, Paris, 1955).

Smith, R. B., *An International History of the Vietnam War, Vol I: Revolution versus Containment 1955–61* (Macmillan, 1983).

Snepp, Frank, *Decent Interval: The American Débâcle in Vietnam and the Fall of Saigon* (Allen Lane, 1980).

Trevelyan, Humphrey, *Worlds Apart* (Macmillan, 1971).

Index*

* With brief details of persons named.